ELIZABETH BARRETT BROWNING

VOLUME IV.

AMS PRESS
NEW YORK

ELIZABETH BARRETT BROWNING

Rome, March, 1859

*From a portrait by Field Talfourd, in the National
Portrait Gallery*

Aurora Leigh
a poem in nine books
Book I to Book IV

ELIZABETH
BARRETT
BROWNING

THOMAS·Y·CROWELL·&
COMPANY·NEW~YORK

THE COMPLETE WORKS

OF

ELIZABETH BARRETT BROWNING

Edited with Introductions and Notes by

CHARLOTTE PORTER AND HELEN A. CLARKE

Editors of Robert Browning's Works, Camberwell
Edition; Authors of " Browning Study
Programmes," etc.

VOLUME IV.

NEW YORK
THOMAS Y. CROWELL & CO.
PUBLISHERS

1900

Library of Congress Cataloging in Publication Data

Browning, Elizabeth (Barrett) 1806-1861.
   The complete works of Elizabeth Barrett Browning.

   Reprint of the 1900 ed.
   CONTENTS: v. 1. Biographical introduction.
Critical introduction. Chronological bibliography.
Battle of the Marathon. Essay on mind. Juvenilia.
Seraphim, and other poems.--v. 2. Romaunt of Margret.
Drama of exile. Lady Geraldine. Vision of poets, and
other poems.--v. 3. Duchess May. Sonnets from the
Portugese. Case Guidi windows. Poems before congress.
--[Etc.]
   I. Porter, Charlotte Endymion, 1859-1942, ed.
II. Clarke, Helen Archibald, d. 1926, ed.

PR4180.F73   821´.8   74-148759
ISBN 0-404-08840-6

Reprinted from the edition of 1900, New York
First AMS edition published in 1973
Manufactured in the United States of America

International Standard Book Number:
Complete Set: 0-404-08840-6
Volume 4: 0-404-08844-9

AMS PRESS INC.
NEW YORK, N. Y.   10003

CONTENTS.

———

CRITICAL INTRODUCTION.

INVENTION, historical atmosphere, thought, emotional fire, and wonderful poetic diction are all flung with lavish hand by our poet into this masterpiece of her mature powers. As Gabriel Sarrazin says in his appreciation of Elizabeth Barrett Browning, "in the midst of her poems, several of which are stars of the first magnitude, the romance-poem of 'Aurora Leigh' shines like a sun."

She herself avows her purpose in writing this poem in a letter to Robert Browning already cited in a former introduction, and we take the liberty of quoting it in full here :

"But my chief *intention* just now is the writing of a sort of novel-poem, a poem as completely modern as 'Geraldine's Courtship,' running into the midst of our conventions, and rushing into drawing-rooms and the like, 'where angels fear to tread;' and so, meeting face to face and without mask the Humanity of the age, and speaking the truth as I conceive of it out plainly. That is my intention. It is not mature enough yet to be called a plan. I am waiting for a story, and I won't take one, because I want to make one, and I like to make my own stories, because then I can take liberties with them in the treatment."

Accordingly we find this boldest of poets starting off upon her new adventure about 1852, with a plot evolved out of her own inner consciousness. The bare events of the story might be related in half a dozen sentences. They are perhaps not very unusual in themselves, but they lead to several fine dramatic situations, and, furthermore, could not be better ones as a framework to show up mid-century Victorian England, and thus to give the poet the opportunity of expressing, through her artist heroine, her own opinions and feelings upon the social tendencies of the time, and upon the art-questions that burned always within her soul.

If Matthew Arnold's definition of poetry be accepted, namely, that poetry should be a criticism of life and should be distinguished by high seriousness, then this poem may be said to attain to the highest expression possible in the art. There can be little doubt of the truth of Matthew Arnold's dictum if it be rightly understood to mean not didactic subjective criticism, but the sort of criticism that sympathizes with and interprets and presents life in the garments of living reality. Judged by purist standards, "Aurora Leigh" is faulty in its art because of its commingling of these two sorts of criticism of life. The poet is constantly expressing her opinions through Aurora's lips, at the same time that the life lived in the poem is portrayed with dramatic force, and is entirely outside of the poet's own experiences. On this account Aurora hardly takes hold of one with the grip of a living personality, but seems for one space like the Aurora of the poem, and for another space like the Elizabeth outside of the poem.

To criticise the poem on this score is, however, not altogether fair, since Mrs. Browning had in mind in writing the poem just such a combination, as shown by her acknowledgment in a letter to Mrs. Jameson, that she had put much of herself into it, — " I mean to say, of my soul, my thoughts, emotions, opinions ; in other respects there is not a personal line, of course. It's a sort of poetic art novel. If it's a failure there will be the comfort of having made a worthy effort, of having done it as well as I could." Criticism, accordingly, should be upon how well she has done what she tried to do, though it be admitted that the conception does not fulfil the strictest requirements of art. The same sort of fault may be laid at the door of George Meredith when he hits upon one of his characters as the mouthpiece of his own wise sayings, as he is fond of doing. Besides, what is the author, bursting with thoughts, to do ? He must either thrust his own personality forward, and, like a *deus ex machina*, talk about everything that goes on, or he must incarnate himself in one of his characters in order to gain an opportunity of holding forth.

While the story is certainly such as to aid the poet in her purposes of direct subjective criticism, it has also a strong dramatic value, for the incidents and situations are of a nature to bring out the qualities of the individuals who figure in them. And as it is in real life with human beings so it is with the actors in this imaginary life-drama, they do not and cannot control events, which seem often as if they were in the hands of some perfectly irresponsible world-spirit, yet they may and do control their attitude toward events, making them the means of the unfolding of their own character.

Aurora herself is, of course, the centre around which the story revolves. She introduces us to herself as a lonely child of intense spiritual ardor and with a highly organized artistic temperament, loving beauty both for its own sake and for its part in life as a means of spiritual aspiration.

Unlike many in whom the artistic temperament is the dominating influence, she has keen intellectual perceptions and a power of incisive criticism not unmixed with sarcasm, that show her at once to belong to the period of modern development in womanhood. What could be more delicious than her scornful way of hitting off the absurdities of the education her aunt saw fit to give her, a sort of conglomerate of useless facts and more useless accomplishments!

From the first Aurora is one who thinks and decides for herself and insists upon a woman's right to her own individual growth. As her environment had not conduced to any such attitude we must conclude that it was born in her, and more than one woman can set her seal to the truth of this possibility of being born with a free soul. It is thus the *Zeit Geist* moves onwards. Opinion, force, nothing can stop it.

On the other hand is Romney, fine in character, noble in his intentions, and filled with modern notions of reform; but like the majority of men, even of liberal ideals, there is one little corner of his nature into which the light of progress has never penetrated. He does not, in fact, cannot, because the bias of his nature is so strong, think of woman in any light but as a complement to man. He is incapable of placing himself at the point of view of a woman; and realizing that being, in very truth, a human creature like himself, and not simply a domesticated animal, though society has done its best to make her such, she feels the same impulse as he to expand those intellectual and artistic germs planted within her, as surely as they are within him, and recognizes that she has as inalienable a right as he to her own individual growth.

The coming together of two such natures as these, so alike in their essential qualities of inherent goodness and nobleness, yet so unlike in their external mental trappings, could be productive of nothing but disaster, as is proved when Romney ventures to ask Aurora to marry him.

With that lack of logic so inexplicable in men of his type, he reëchoes all the wise old saws, — as old in spirit as the days of Hesiod, — as to the purely personal nature of womanly sympathy, woman's lack of power to generalize, and then demands from Aurora sympathy in all his undertakings and help in carrying them out. Yet he does not propose to give her the smallest grain of sympathy in her art aspirations, partly because he does not think art is woman's sphere, and partly because he puts the ideal of social reform above all others, and expects his wife to submit immediately to his superior judgment. The clear-seeing woman-soul of Aurora is injured to the core by a love so proffered. It seems to her that it cannot be love at all that is so disregardful of the nature and aspirations of the one beloved, and that seems bent so entirely upon subjecting her to his own uses and interests.

This conflict of two souls Mrs. Browning has presented with consummate power, bringing out fully the masculine egotism of Romney — so abnormal as to amount to under-developed consciousness — and the awakening feminine egotism of Aurora, which though it is aware of its own needs and rights does not question those of men, and in doing so presents a more highly developed phase of consciousness. The conflict of Romney and Aurora is prophetic of the struggle which is everywhere going on to-day between the deep-seated unconscious egotism of men and the awakening, enlightened egotism of women. It remains to be seen whether such chastening as Romney received will be the means of awakening in men a higher consciousness, or whether it must needs be left in the hands of the *Zeit Geist* to endow coming generations with it at their birth.

Aurora's criticisms of Romney's methods of reform also have a larger significance than belongs simply to the story. At the time when Mrs. Browning was writing, socialistic schemes for the regeneration of society were filling the air. Fourier's communistic theories made a wide appeal to the conscience of awakening humanitarianism, his influence being felt in America not only in the famous Brook Farm coöperative experiment in New England, but in the establishment by the Frenchman Cabet of Phalansteries on the banks of the Mississippi. All these experiments turned out failures, and the keen-sighted Aurora perhaps put her finger upon the very kernel of their weakness when she exclaimed :

> ". . . Ah, your Fouriers failed,
> Because not poets enough to understand
> That life develops from within." . . .

She felt instinctively that the whole of humanity could not be fitted into a social framework which allowed of no individual expansion. Not but that such schemes always claim to be for the best freedom of the individual, but they are too often dominated by some especial bias as to what constitutes freedom, from which it follows that those desiring a different sort of freedom are as much handicapped as ever.

Another point she criticises in Romney's schemes is his concentration upon the material aspects of life. He is bent merely upon alleviating physical conditions, contending that they must be changed before any spiritual or artistic development is possible, while Aurora insists that the cultivation of the spiritual and artistic nature must go hand in hand with the better-ment of physical condition — a truth which we believe the more thoughtful of reformers have come to recognize to-day.

For these two, each so strongly grounded in his own opinion, there could be no compromise, and each must perforce take up the burden of life alone. She must work out her destiny by means of the art that has taken possession of her being, he through his plans for remoulding and bettering society. How fanatical and narrow a man may become in his vision when he is the victim of one idea, however praiseworthy his intentions, is well brought out when he denies love itself in his decision to marry a child of the people for whom he has only a universal sort of affection, and so to unite the upper and lower classes of society.

Among the most beautiful episodes of the poem are those that tell of Marian, whose early life Aurora describes with passionate sympathy, illuminating Marian's crude account with all the warmth of her poetic nature. Marian is one of those blossoms of purity and goodness — the prototype perhaps of Robert Browning's Pompilia — that sometimes spring from the mud and scum of degraded surroundings. She is in herself enough to prove that the seeds of spirituality and beauty are latent everywhere, budding forth in places least suspected, and that the appeal to such latent possibilities in humanity would be worth a great deal, as Aurora believed, in the process of remoulding society. It is true she is a child of the imagination, but the workers at the dismal ends of cities will tell you that she is no unreal creation.

It is characteristic of Romney that it never enters his head to help Marian enlarge her stock of knowledge, though any one might have seen with half an eye that a girl who had cherished stray leaves from the poets and novelists given to her by wayside peddlers might have possibilities for intellectual development as well as for work among the poor. As in the case of Aurora, he only wanted her to help him in his life work, and act as a sort of symbol, through his marriage with her, of his pet social theories.

The poet very cleverly shows the uselessness of the marriage as helping along in any way the realization of Romney's optimistic hopes for society, by the criticisms she puts into the mouth of Lord Howe in the scene in the church before the projected marriage. He likens the poor to a superannuated, brutalized King Lear, and the privileged classes to the king's daughters Regan and Goneril, the two having become so far separated that they can never be brought together again by any such external means as Romney proposes. The realization that the rich owe their privilege to the defrauding of the poor implied in this comparison shows how clearly our poet saw the true relations between rich and poor ; but though Lord Howe perceives it, and deplores it, he is too much of his own class to see any practicable way of righting the injustice. He is sure Romney has not found it, and very properly calls him a mad Hamlet acting a play of love in order to show society its own evil doing. This scene in the church is one of the most dramatic bits in the whole poem. The scraps of conversation that fall from the assembled guests reflect admirably the social tone. It has been criticised, of course, as not true to life, but no one who has attended fashionable functions with a soul somewhat above them but will recognize in this shallow gathering the veritable seal of so-called high society, interested in its own little social events and with about as much consciousness as children of the true bearings of social problems ; and just as there will always be some people of true culture even in high society, Lord Howe and Aurora herself may be taken to represent that element.

Aurora's life in the meantime has been one of laborious work at her art, but though she has not attained her ideal, she has not weakened any in her opinions as to the importance of art and her own calling to it. But her lonely life is producing its effect upon her character.

With subtle touches the poet shows how the need of human love is deepening in her being, and how though she will not whisper it to her own inmost thoughts, her heart yearns towards Romney. Even Lady Waldemar's confession to Aurora of her own love for Romney brings no tell-tale admission from Aurora. The indications of her growing feeling are shown in her apathy in regard to Marian, after her first cousinly action in going to see the young girl, and with perfect good faith accepting this child of the people as worthy to be united with a Leigh. If she had been a little less occupied with her own feelings, had not been, for example, so haunted by Romney's " good-night " when he bade her farewell after their walk home from Marian's —

> ". . . like good-night
> Beside a deathbed, where the morrow's sun
> Is sure to come too late for more good days,"

she would have been more suspicious of Lady Waldemar's intentions in regard to Marian.   That lady had
certainly revealed herself as an unscrupulous person
in her proposals for postponing the wedding ; and
Aurora, by rights, should have shown a little more care
for Marian's welfare.   Aurora knows all this, afterwards, and blames herself when the projected wedding
ends in such a disastrous fiasco.

The climax of the church scene is reached when
Romney makes his announcement from the altar, and
there comes the sudden revulsion from the light tone
of the privileged, selfish, and thoughtless to the savage
roar of the mob ; the poor showing themselves in their
unseemly rage and violence no better qualified to judge
of Romney and his motives than the rich in their
frivolous indifference.

These events throw Aurora and Romney together
again, but the time is not yet ripe for the consumma-
tion of their understanding of each other.   Though
Aurora now knows in her own heart that she loves
him, the attitude toward her art which he still persists
in is exasperating both to her pride and her intellect.

Romney's lesson in relation to Marian has but
taught him that perhaps it is better to succeed in a very
small aim like Aurora's than to fail in a great aim like
his own.   She at least has

> " . . . helped the facile youth to live youth's day
>   With innocent distraction, still perhaps
>   Suggestive of things better than her rhymes,"

while he has succeeded only in ruining one whom he
would have helped, like an imperfectly trained sheep
dog, "Who bites the kids through too much zeal."
He is not yet ready to admit that art can have any

serious purpose in life, especially a woman's art; the worn, weary, and heart-sick Aurora, she who has put her life-blood into her work and chosen poverty that she might devote herself to its perfecting, is supposed, as she feels in anguish, "a thing too small to deign to know." Pitifully she gives voice to her mood in the closing lines of the Fourth Book :

> "He blew me, plainly, from the crucible
> As some intruding, interrupting fly,
> Not worth the pains of his analysis
> Absorbed on nobler subjects. Hurt a fly !
> He would not for the world : he's pitiful
> To flies even. 'Sing,' says he, 'and tease me still,
> If that's your way, poor insect.' "   . . .

Aurora, left to herself again, still continues to develop her artistic powers.   In the fine opening lines of the Fifth Book we hear the poet's own voice in one of her compelling moods, when it seems as if words dropped down upon her from some super-earthly realm, so rare and choice are they.   She is describing what the poet's inspiration must be to take hold of and keep the heart of humanity :

> ". . . Shall I hope
> To speak my poems in mysterious tune
> With man and nature? — with a lava-lymph
> That trickles from successive galaxies
> Still drop by drop adown the finger of God
> In still new worlds? — with summer-days in this
> That scarce dare breathe they are so beautiful?
> With spring's delicious trouble in the ground,
> Tormented by the quickened blood of roots,
> And softly pricked by golden crocus-sheaves
> In token of the harvest-time of flowers?
> With winters and with autumns, — and beyond
> With human heart's large seasons, when it hopes
> And fears, joys, grieves, and loves? — with all that strain

> Of sexual passion, which devours the flesh
> In a sacrament of souls? with mother's breasts
> Which, round the new-made creatures hanging there,
> Throb luminous and harmonious like pure spheres? —
> With multitudinous life, and finally
> With the great escapings of ecstatic souls,
> Who, in a rush of too long prisoned flame,
> Their radiant faces upward, burn away
> This dark of the body, issuing on a world
> Beyond our mortal? — can I speak my verse
> So plainly in tune to these things and the rest
> That men shall feel it catch them on the quick
> As having the same warrant over them
> To hold and move them if they will or no,
> Alike imperious as the primal rhythm
> Of that theurgic nature?" .   .   .

By her failures Aurora learns to reach out toward
the highest, most human planes of art.   She discovers
the inadequacy of pure nature-poetry.   Nature described for its own sake is null.   She has awakened to
the fact —

> "   .   .   .   There's not a flower of spring
> That dies ere June but vaunts itself allied
> By issue and symbol, by significance
> And correspondence, to that spirit-world
> Outside the limits of our space and time,
> Whereto we are bound.   Let poets give it voice
> With human meanings, — else they miss the thought."

Her own pastoral poem taught her this.   She distrusts,
too, the poet who trundles back his soul five hundred
years —

> " Past moat and drawbridge, into a castle court
> To sing — oh, not of lizard or of toad
> Alive i' the ditch there, — 'twere excusable,
> But of some black chief, half knight, half sheep-lifter."

The poet's true work, she declares, is to picture his
own times, to grasp the palpitating human life of the

present replete with fuller passion and meaning than it
could be in the so-called days of romance. This
whole passage gains in interest when we regard it as
an expression of our poet's own artistic creed, and
reflects the independence of spirit with which she was
dowered when so many of the poets of the Victorian
era have shown a decided proneness for trundling back
into the past.

Fine as this artistic creed is, and true as it is, it does
not state the whole truth. It has that narrowness of
vision which belongs to any mind in the flood-tide of
a new conviction. In days when the fiat has gone
forth that romance is dead, and poetry sunk forever
beneath the dull level of common sense materialism, it
requires strong statements to convince the Classicist
and the Romanticist that the Modern has any artistic
rights at all, and if they be knocked down for a little,
while the Modern vindicates itself, no great harm is
done ; for presently the larger vision must come. Then
it will be seen that the true mission of art is to resus-
citate the life of the past as well as to record the life
of the present, and that even to tell an old myth over
again in exquisite form such as a Tennyson or a Morris
may command is to put new beauty, which is to put
new life, into a myth.

Aurora, however, is in such a revolutionary frame of
mind that she dares to question the necessity for a
drama being in five acts. Why not ten, or seven, or
fifteen — any number that will unfold the passion
properly. Perhaps if she had been familiar with the
Hindu play, "The Mrichchhakati," with what seems
like an unconscionable number of acts, she might have
been convinced that the charm of a drama, like that of
a sonnet, grows out of the very fact that the necessity

of developing your thought or your passion within a certain limit strengthens and intensifies that thought or that passion either by condensing it or by suggesting more than can be said.

For some reason or another the human mind is in sympathy with definite boundaries, and no matter how often it may go astray and think itself in love with sprangling indefinite art forms, and imagine that by means of them it can better express its strivings after the infinite, it will find that after all expression is richer and fuller if confined within bounds, and that the infinite is better suggested thus than through the attempted limitless in form.

The thought that the drama may some day outgrow the conventions of the actual stage, and take for its stage the human soul, reminds the reader at once of Robert Browning's unique and original adventures in his poetry, only a small proportion of which conforms to the accepted dramatic form, yet the whole of it so instinct with dramatic reality. He had the wisdom, however, not to attempt such formless dramas as Aurora advocates, but to create for himself in his dramatic monologues a form with its own laws of organic unity just as surely as the old drama had its laws.

One seems to see Robert, too, in the poet Graham, whose breadth of style she never envied. A style

> " Which gives you, with a random smutch or two
> (Near-sighted critics analyse to smutch),
> Such delicate perspectives of full life."

Does this not hit off neatly Browning's massive way of sketching in a character without any circumlocutory descriptions of mere externals ? If any doubt remains as to Browning's being meant, this domestic touch ought to settle it. She confesses she envies Graham —

"Because you have a wife who loves you so,
 She half forgets, at moments, to be proud
 Of being Graham's wife, until a friend observes,
 'The boy here has his father's massive brow
 Done small in wax . . . if we push back the curls.'"

In the same way, Belmore, whom she admires for his unity of aim,

". . . to which he cuts his cedarn poems, fine
 As sketchers do their pencils," . . .

suggests Tennyson, and Mark Gage with his

". . . caressing colour and trancing tone
 Whereby you're swept away and melted in
 The sensual element," . . .

suggests Swinburne.

A rich, human note winds itself in and out of all these ruminations upon art. Aurora is the artist consumed with the flames of creative impulse burning toward some wholly worthy accomplishment, yet she is the woman, distrustful of her powers, and longing for the appreciation and sympathy of the man whom she loves. Angry at herself for this woman's weakness, she decides with a right woman's manliness to crush out her desire for approbation, and to strive to the uttermost for the attainment of her highest purposes, — to screw her courage to the sticking-place, and if she fail, she fails ; at least the failure will be an honorable one.

She had need of all her bravery to withstand the blow which befalls her in the report of Lady Waldemar's coming marriage to Romney.

The interlude of Lord Howe's evening, where Aurora hears this painful news, gives us another interesting glimpse into the social world, and breaks what might otherwise have proved the subjective monotony of this, the Fifth Book. Lady Waldemar appears before us in all her social radiance, while in Smith and Sir Blaise Delorme are sketched for us two diverse types of the times, — the devout churchman and the Germanized liberal, whose opinions smack of the extremes of socialism. Their conversation about Lady Waldemar is highly entertaining to the reader as an exhibition of human variousness, but is not exactly exhilarating for poor Aurora, who is further tortured by Lord Howe when he uses his kindly offices in behalf of a man who wants to marry her. The last straw is Lady Waldemar herself, who flaunts her intimacy with Romney in Aurora's face.

This brings things to a crisis with Aurora. What is there left for her to do but go back to her childhood's Italy ?

The passage through Paris on the way to Italy gives the poet a chance to express her opinion at some length upon French character and art. Penetrating and wise are these remarks ; but one begins to chafe a little at what seems to be the degeneration of the poem into a mere critical essay, when the human interest comes uppermost again in the discovery of Marian.

The poet is always supreme when she is describing Marian, and Marian the mother is even more exquisitely lovely than Marian the child and Marian the sewing-girl. Aurora herself appears at a decided disadvantage in comparison — irritating because of her priggishness in relation to Marian. Her superior virtue and her moralizing strike a harsh note, and even after the whole truth of the terrible tale has become known to her, she makes somewhat too much of the perfectly self-evident fact that Marian is pure. This might be used as an argument against those who think Aurora is body and soul Mrs. Browning. She must have had larger sympathies than her own Aurora, or she could not have produced the impression of Marian's superiority just here.

From here on the human interest deepens, and there is something like the thickening of a plot in Aurora's misunderstanding of Vincent Carrington's letter, and her failure to receive Lord Howe's letter, which, when Romney and herself come together for the third time, causes them to talk at cross purposes and entangle themselves in a bewildering series of misunderstandings. This gives an opportunity for several fine dramatic denouements. Though Aurora's understanding of the situation is all at fault, and she is constantly in a state between surprise and indignation at Romney's evident desire to make her understand how much he loves her, they find themselves for the first time in accord intellectually. Romney has finally been conquered by her last book and admits that it has spoken to him, not personally as an utterance of hers, but from outside herself as veritable universal truth. It has brought home to him for the first time the conviction that there is an interdependence of the physical and the spiritual. He sees now that his own failure has come partly because he would not recognize the need of cultivating the spiritual side of those whom he would help materially, and partly through his own arrogance in supposing that with his strong arm he could remake society and set all things in the universe right by forcibly putting the degraded members of the community in an environment entirely uncongenial to their undeveloped natures, and expecting them to like it and thrive under it. His

mood now is almost one of *laissez faire*, but Aurora
shows him that though no human being can do much,
yet their feeblest efforts toward the right tell in the
great sum of human endeavor.

She, too, confesses that her success in her art seems
only like a failure to her, because she realizes that love
is a greater thing than art.   The situation here is a
poignant one for the lovers.   Now that all barriers
between their souls are down, the "stern daughter of
the voice of God," Duty, must separate them forever.

A crescendo of climaxes now hurries the poem to
a close.   The first is when the truth that Lady Waldemar is not Romney's wife at last comes out, and
Aurora's momentary relief is cruelly broken by Romney's announcement that he considers himself bound
to Marian.   The second is when Marian joins them
upon the terrace and, rising to a glorious height, hardly
of this world, so intense is its spirituality, she refuses
Romney's offer of marriage upon grounds that crown
her as the one truly intuitively lofty soul of the poem
— she who had no theories of art or life, but reached
out instinctively toward the high and noble in action,
as when a little child she sought to feast her eyes upon
the wideness of the sky.   The final climax is when
Aurora discovers that Romney is blind, and at last confesses her love for him.

It is a misfortune that even in the ecstasy of their
acknowledged love, after so many torturing years to
both of them, the poet makes them drop into theoriz-
ing again and finally settle up the affairs of society and
what their relation to it is to be.

Still we can forgive this in view of the fact that
with the exception of "The Sonnets from the Portu-
guese" there are no passages in any poet that reflect

such an exalted and wondrous moment of love as those
at the end of " Aurora Leigh " —

"But oh, the night! oh, bitter-sweet! oh, sweet!
O dark, O moon and stars, O ecstasy
Of darkness!   O great mystery of love,
In which absorbed, loss, anguish, treason's self
Enlarges rapture — as a pebble dropped
In some full wine-cup overbrims the wine!
While we two sat together, leaned that night
So close my very garments crept and thrilled
With strange electric life, and both my cheeks
Grew red, then pale, with touches from my hair
In which his breath was,— while the golden moon
Was hung before our faces as the badge
Of some sublime inherited despair,
Since ever to be seen by only one,—
A voice said, low and rapid as a sigh,
Yet breaking, I felt conscious, from a smile,
'Thank God, who made me blind, to make me see!
Shine on, Aurora, dearest light of souls,
Which rul'st for evermore both day and night!
I am happy.'
            I flung closer to his breast,
As sword that, after battle, flings to sheath;
And, in that hurtle of united souls,
The mystic motions which in common moods
Are shut beyond our sense, broke in on us,
And, as we sat, we felt the old earth spin,
And all the starry turbulence of worlds
Swing round us in their audient circles, till,
If that same golden moon were overhead
Or if beneath our feet, we did not know."

Some one has said that this poem is a splendid failure, but it would be nearer the truth to say that it is
a triumph, which no defects in artistic construction
can dim.   It is true that the poet's proneness to
criticise and theorize is often in danger of upsetting
the artistic balance of the whole.   No idea comes into
her mind that she does not immediately elaborate a

scroll work of secondary ideas around it, and it frequently happens that the same thought is enlarged upon more than once ; but, on the other hand, no criticism was ever before clothed in such living, inspired language.   Every time a thought recurs it is burned in afresh with symbol and metaphor, as when a jewel is made to show different qualities by fresh settings. Her command of expression is indeed marvellous, and with successive readings her beauties of style impress themselves more and more.

Aurora being the philosopher of the poem, it is principally in connection with her that the too much talking is felt, though Romney sometimes evinces a tendency in the same direction.   This, however, applies only to their intellectual aspect.   On the human side Aurora especially is admirably managed, and stands as a faithful and sympathetic portrayal of what we may venture to call the pioneer "new woman," who has not quite freed herself from the inheritances of the past. So strenuous for her individuality at the start, she is ready to sink it in her love at the end.   She had not learned that only by the highest reverence for her own individuality could she love properly.   However, as Romney had learned to respect her individuality, she could afford to be generous in her first love-raptures.

This slight reactionary movement on her part is also illustrated in her statement that women would better show what they can do instead of asking for suffrage, as if women ever could show what they might do fully unless freed of all disabilities, and furthermore as if they would ever get full credit for what they do without the recognition by the state of their equality. What they need is both, Aurora !

In fact, the final summing up in the poem is on

the whole reactionary in thought.   Nobody's theories seem to receive vindication, and Romney and Aurora give one the impression that they will take up their work for humanity upon the old charitable principles instead of upon the larger principles of the development and reorganization of society.   It did not follow because Romney's methods were wrong that therefore his principles were wrong, nor because Fourier was " void " that no saner methods for raising the masses might not be evolved.

The vindication, however, comes in the full blossoming of Romney's and Aurora's characters.   Both attain the uplands of human growth in their willingness to sacrifice their personal feelings for higher, less selfish motives, and they receive their just reward, because the poet is not going to let her Marian fail by taking any lower ground than they.   Thus, in the unfolding and final exaltation of human character, the poet has crowned her art.

One wonders whether the final denouement required that Romney should have lost his sight.   He certainly had not been so wicked as to deserve such a horrible punishment, and surely Aurora's book would have been just as convincing if he had been able to read it himself ; besides, it reminds one of the hero of " Jane Eyre," as more than one critic has remarked. That blindness of Romney's seems to hang over one during the rest of life, like a personal grief.   Perhaps the sorrow one feels over it is its justification !   Be that as it may, it gives scope to the poet for some very beautiful lines, and we will accept any event at her hands for the sake of her impassioned eloquence in portraying it.

As for the minor characters, their sketching in is

masterly, as we have indicated in passing, and they reveal, as nothing else Mrs. Browning has done, her talent for creation in the purely human dramatic field.

One chief character we have not mentioned, and of him we leave it to Swinburne to speak fittingly :

"The piercing and terrible pathos of the story is as incomparable and as irresistible as the divine expression of womanly and motherly rapture which seems to suffuse and imbue the very page, the very print, with the radiance and the fragrance of babyhood. There never was, and there never will be, such another baby in type as that. Other poets, even of the inferior sex, have paid immortal tribute to the immortal Godhead incarnate in the mortal and transitory presence of infancy ; the homage of one or two among them, a Homer or a Hugo, may have been worthy to be mistaken for a mother's ; but here is a mother's indeed ; and 'the yearlong creature' so divinely described must live in sight of all her readers as long as human nature, or as English poetry, survives. No words can ever be adequate to give thanks for such a gift as this."

CHARLOTTE PORTER.
HELEN A. CLARKE.

AURORA LEIGH.

A POEM IN NINE BOOKS.

1856.

DEDICATION

TO

JOHN KENYON, Esq.

THE words " cousin " and " friend " are constantly recurring in this poem, the last pages of which have been finished under the hospitality of your roof, my own dearest cousin and friend ; — cousin and friend, in a sense of less equality and greater disinterestedness than " Romney " 's.

Ending, therefore, and preparing once more to quit England, I venture to leave in your hands this book, the most mature of my works, and the one into which my highest convictions upon Life and Art have entered ; that as, through my various efforts in Literature and steps in life, you have believed in me, borne with me, and been generous to me, far beyond the common uses of mere relationship or sympathy of mind, so you may kindly accept, in sight of the public, this poor sign of esteem, gratitude, and affection from — Your unforgetting

E. B. B.

39 DEVONSHIRE PLACE :
October 17, 1856.

AURORA LEIGH.

FIRST BOOK.

OF writing many books there is no end ;
And I who have written much in prose and verse
For others' uses, will write now for mine, —
Will write my story for my better self,
As when you paint your portrait for a friend,
Who keeps it in a drawer and looks at it
Long after he has ceased to love you, just
To hold together what he was and is.
I, writing thus, am still what men call young ;
I have not so far left the coasts of life   10
To travel inward, that I cannot hear
That murmur of the outer Infinite
Which unweaned babies smile at in their sleep
When wondered at for smiling ; not so far,
But still I catch my mother at her post
Beside the nursery door, with finger up,
" Hush, hush — here's too much noise ! " while her
          sweet eyes
Leap forward, taking part against her word
In the child's riot.   Still I sit and feel   19
My father's slow hand, when she had left us both,
Stroke out my childish curls across his knee,
And hear Assunta's daily jest (she knew
He liked it better than a better jest)
Inquire how many golden scudi went
To make such ringlets.   O my father's hand,
Stroke heavily, heavily the poor hair down,
Draw, press the child's head closer to thy knee !
I'm still too young, too young, to sit alone.

I write.   My mother was a Florentine,
Whose rare blue eyes were shut from seeing me   30
When scarcely I was four years old, my life
A poor spark snatched up from a failing lamp
Which went out therefore.   She was weak and frail ;
She could not bear the joy of giving life,
The mother's rapture slew her.   If her kiss
Had left a longer weight upon my lips
It might have steadied the uneasy breath,
And reconciled and fraternised my soul
With the new order.   As it was, indeed,
I felt a mother-want about the world,   40
And still went seeking, like a bleating lamb
Left out at night in shutting up the fold, —
As restless as a nest-deserted bird
Grown chill through something being away, though
      what
It knows not.   I, Aurora Leigh, was born
To make my father sadder, and myself
Not overjoyous, truly.   Women know
The way to rear up children (to be just),
They know a simple, merry, tender knack
Of tying sashes, fitting baby-shoes,   50
And stringing pretty words that make no sense,
And kissing full sense into empty words,
Which things are corals to cut life upon,
Although such trifles : children learn by such,
Love's holy earnest in a pretty play
And get not over-early solemnised,
But seeing, as in a rose-bush, Love's Divine
Which burns and hurts not, — not a single bloom, —
Become aware and unafraid of Love.
Such good do mothers.   Fathers love as well   60
— Mine did, I know, — but still with heavier brains,

And wills more consciously responsible,
And not as wisely, since less foolishly ;
So mothers have God's license to be missed.

My father was an austere Englishman,
Who, after a dry lifetime spent at home
In college-learning, law, and parish talk,
Was flooded with a passion unaware,
His whole provisioned and complacent past   69
Drowned out from him that moment.   As he stood
In Florence, where he had come to spend a month
And note the secret of Da Vinci's drains,
He musing somewhat absently perhaps
Some English question . . . whether men should pay
The unpopular but necessary tax
With left or right hand — in the alien sun
In that great square of the Santissima
There drifted past him (scarcely marked enough
To move his comfortable island scorn)
A train of priestly banners, cross and psalm,   80
The white-veiled rose-crowned maidens holding up
Tall tapers, weighty for such wrists, aslant
To the blue luminous tremor of the air,
And letting drop the white wax as they went
To eat the bishop's wafer at the church ;
From which long trail of chanting priests and girls,
A face flashed like a cymbal on his face
And shook with silent clangour brain and heart,
Transfiguring him to music.   Thus, even thus,
He too received his sacramental gift   90
With eucharistic meanings ; for he loved.

And thus beloved, she died.   I've heard it said
That but to see him in the first surprise

Of widower and father, nursing me,
Unmothered little child of four years old,
His large man's hands afraid to touch my curls,
As if the gold would tarnish, — his grave lips
Contriving such a miserable smile
As if he knew needs must, or I should die,   99
And yet 'twas hard, — would almost make the stones
Cry out for pity. There's a verse he set
In Santa Croce to her memory, —
"Weep for an infant too young to weep much
When death removed this mother" — stops the mirth
To-day on women's faces when they walk
With rosy children hanging on their gowns,
Under the cloister to escape the sun
That scorches in the piazza. After which
He left our Florence and made haste to hide
Himself, his prattling child, and silent grief,   110
Among the mountains above Pelago;
Because unmothered babes, he thought, had need
Of mother nature more than others use,
And Pan's white goats, with udders warm and full
Of mystic contemplations, come to feed
Poor milkless lips of orphans like his own —
Such scholar-scraps he talked, I've heard from friends,
For even prosaic men who wear grief long
Will get to wear it as a hat aside   119
With a flower stuck in't. Father, then, and child,
We lived among the mountains many years,
God's silence on the outside of the house,
And we who did not speak too loud within,
And old Assunta to make up the fire,
Crossing herself whene'er a sudden flame
Which lightened from the firewood, made alive
That picture of my mother on the wall.

The painter drew it after she was dead,
And when the face was finished, throat and hands,
Her cameriera carried him, in hate   130
Of the English-fashioned shroud, the last brocade
She dressed in at the Pitti ; " he should paint
No sadder thing than that," she swore, " to wrong
Her poor signora."   Therefore very strange
The effect was.   I, a little child, would crouch
For hours upon the floor with knees drawn up,
And gaze across them, half in terror, half
In adoration, at the picture there, —
That swan-like supernatural white life
Just sailing upward from the red stiff silk   140
Which seemed to have no part in it nor power
To keep it from quite breaking out of bounds.
For hours I sat and stared.   Assunta's awe
And my poor father's melancholy eyes
Still pointed that way.   That way went my thoughts
When wandering beyond sight.   And as I grew
In years, I mixed, confused, unconsciously,
Whatever I last read or heard or dreamed,
Abhorrent, admirable, beautiful,
Pathetical, or ghastly, or grotesque,   150
With still that face . . . which did not therefore
      change,
But kept the mystic level of all forms,
Hates, fears, and admirations, was by turns
Ghost, fiend, and angel, fairy, witch, and sprite,
A dauntless Muse who eyes a dreadful Fate,
A loving Psyche who loses sight of Love,
A still Medusa with mild milky brows
All curdled and all clothed upon with snakes
Whose slime falls fast as sweat will ; or anon
Our Lady of the Passion, stabbed with swords   160

Where the Babe sucked ; or Lamia in her first
Moonlighted pallor, ere she shrunk and blinked
And shuddering wriggled down to the unclean ;
Or my own mother, leaving her last smile
In her last kiss upon the baby-mouth
My father pushed down on the bed for that, —
Or my dead mother, without smile or kiss,
Buried at Florence.   All which images,
Concentred on the picture, glassed themselves
Before my meditative childhood, as   170
The incoherencies of change and death
Are represented fully, mixed and merged,
In the smooth fair mystery of perpetual Life.
And while I stared away my childish wits
Upon my mother's picture (ah, poor child !),
My father, who through love had suddenly
Thrown off the old.conventions, broken loose
From chin-bands of the soul, like Lazarus,
Yet had no time to learn to talk and walk
Or grow anew familiar with the sun, —   180
Who had reached to freedom, not to action, lived,
But lived as one entranced, with thoughts, not aims,—
Whom love had unmade from a common man
But not completed to an uncommon man, —
My father taught me what he had learnt the best
Before he died and left me, — grief and love.
And, seeing we had books among the hills,
Strong words of counselling souls confederate
With vocal pines and waters, — out of books
He taught me all the ignorance of men,   190
And how God laughs in heaven when any man
Says " Here I'm learned ; this, I understand ;
In that, I am never caught at fault or doubt.''
He sent the schools to school, demonstrating

A fool will pass for such through one mistake,
While a philosopher will pass for such,
Through said mistakes being ventured in the gross
And heaped up to a system.
                                   I am like,
They tell me, my dear father.   Broader brows
Howbeit, upon a slenderer undergrowth   200
Of delicate features, — paler, near as grave ;
But then my mother's smile breaks up the whole,
And makes it better sometimes than itself.
So, nine full years, our days were hid with God
Among his mountains : I was just thirteen,
Still growing like the plants from unseen roots
In tongue-tied Springs, — and suddenly awoke
To full life and life's needs and agonies
With an intense, strong, struggling heart beside
A stone-dead father.   Life, struck sharp on death, 210
Makes awful lightning.   His last word was " Love — "
" Love, my child, love, love ! " — (then he had
     done with grief)
" Love, my child."   Ere I answered he was gone,
And none was left to love in all the world.

There, ended childhood.   What succeeded next
I recollect as, after fevers, men
Thread back the passage of delirium,
Missing the turn still, baffled by the door ;
Smooth endless days, notched here and there with
     knives,
A weary, wormy darkness, spurred i' the flank   220
With flame, that it should eat and end itself
Like some tormented scorpion.   Then at last
I do remember clearly how there came
A stranger with authority, not right

(I thought not), who commanded, caught me up
From old Assunta's neck ; how, with a shriek,
She let me go, —while I, with ears too full
Of my father's silence to shriek back a word,
In all a child's astonishment at grief   229
Stared at the wharf-edge where she stood and moaned,
My poor Assunta, where she stood and moaned !
The white walls, the blue hills, my Italy,
Drawn backward from the shuddering steamer-deck,
Like one in anger drawing back her skirts
Which suppliants catch at.   Then the bitter sea
Inexorably pushed between us both
And, sweeping up the ship with my despair,
Threw us out as a pasture to the stars.

Ten nights and days we voyaged on the deep ;
Ten nights and days without the common face   240
Of any day or night ; the moon and sun
Cut off from the green reconciling earth,
To starve into a blind ferocity
And glare unnatural ; the very sky
(Dropping its bell-net down upon the sea,
As if no human heart should 'scape alive)
Bedraggled with the desolating salt,
Until it seemed no more that holy heaven
To which my father went.   All new and strange ;
The universe turned stranger, for a child.   250

Then, land ! — then, England ! oh, the frosty cliffs
Looked cold upon me.   Could I find a home
Among those mean red houses through the fog ?
And when I heard my father's language first
From alien lips which had no kiss for mine
I wept aloud, then laughed, then wept, then wept,

And some one near me said the child was mad
Through much sea-sickness. The train swept us on :
Was this my father's England ? the great isle ?
The ground seemed cut up from the fellowship   260
Of verdure, field from field, as man from man ;
The skies themselves looked low and positive,
As almost you could touch them with a hand,
And dared to do it they were so far off
From God's celestial crystals ; all things blurred
And dull and vague. Did Shakespeare and his mates
Absorb the light here ? — not a hill or stone
With heart to strike a radiant colour up
Or active outline on the indifferent air.

I think I see my father's sister stand   270
Upon the hall-step of her country-house
To give me welcome. She stood straight and calm,
Her somewhat narrow forehead braided tight
As if for taming accidental thoughts
From possible pulses ; brown hair pricked with gray
By frigid use of life (she was not old,
Although my father's elder by a year),
A nose drawn sharply, yet in delicate lines ;
A close mild mouth, a little soured about
The ends, through speaking unrequited loves   280
Or peradventure niggardly half-truths ;
Eyes of no colour, — once they might have smiled,
But never, never have forgot themselves
In smiling ; cheeks, in which was yet a rose
Of perished summers, like a rose in a book,
Kept more for ruth than pleasure, — if past bloom,
Past fading also.
                    She had lived, we'll say,
A harmless life, she called a virtuous life,

A quiet life, which was not life at all
(But that, she had not lived enough to know),   290
Between the vicar and the county squires,
The lord-lieutenant looking down sometimes
From the empyrean to assure their souls
Against chance vulgarisms, and, in the abyss,
The apothecary, looked on once a year
To prove their soundness of humility.
The poor-club exercised her Christian gifts
Of knitting stockings, stitching petticoats,
Because we are of one flesh, after all,
And need one flannel (with a proper sense   300
Of difference in the quality) — and still
The book-club, guarded from your modern trick
Of shaking dangerous questions from the crease,
Preserved her intellectual.   She had lived
A sort of cage-bird life, born in a cage,
Accounting that to leap from perch to perch
Was act and joy enough for any bird.
Dear heaven, how silly are the things that live
In thickets, and eat berries !
.   I, alas,   309
A wild bird scarcely fledged, was brought to her cage,
And she was there to meet me.   Very kind.
Bring the clean water, give out the fresh seed.

She stood upon the steps to welcome me,
Calm, in black garb.   I clung about her neck, —
Young babes, who catch at every shred of wool
To draw the new light closer, catch and cling
Less blindly.   In my ears my father's word
Hummed ignorantly, as the sea in shells,
"Love, love, my child."   She, black there with my
      grief,

Might feel my love — she was his sister once —   320
I clung to her.   A moment she seemed moved,
Kissed me with cold lips, suffered me to cling,
And drew me feebly through the hall into
The room she sat in.

               There, with some strange spasm
Of pain and passion, she wrung loose my hands
Imperiously, and held me at arm's length,
And with two grey-steel naked-bladed eyes
Searched through my face, — ay, stabbed it through
    and through,
Through brows and cheeks and chin, as if to find
A wicked murderer in my innocent face,   330
If not here, there perhaps.   Then, drawing breath,
She struggled for her ordinary calm —
And missed it rather, — told me not to shrink,
As if she had told me not to lie or swear, —
" She loved my father and would love me too
As long as I deserved it."   Very kind.

I understood her meaning afterward ;
She thought to find my mother in my face,
And questioned it for that.   For she, my aunt,
Had loved my father truly, as she could,   340
And hated, with the gall of gentle souls,
My Tuscan mother who had fooled away
A wise man from wise courses, a good man
From obvious duties, and, depriving her,
His sister, of the household precedence,
Had wronged his tenants, robbed his native land,
And made him mad, alike by life and death,
In love and sorrow.   She had pored for years
What sort of woman could be suitable
To her sort of hate, to entertain it with,   350

And so, her very curiosity
Became hate too, and all the idealism
She ever used in life was used for hate,
Till hate, so nourished, did exceed at last
The love from which it grew, in strength and heat,
And wrinkled her smooth conscience with a sense
Of disputable virtue (say not, sin)
When Christian doctrine was enforced at church.

And thus my father's sister was to me
My mother's hater.   From that day she did   360
Her duty to me (I appreciate it
In her own word as spoken to herself),
Her duty, in large measure, well pressed out
But measured always.   She was generous, bland,
More courteous than was tender, gave me still
The first place, — as if fearful that God's saints
Would look down suddenly and say "Herein
You missed a point, I think, through lack of love."
Alas, a mother never is afraid
Of speaking angerly to any child,   370
Since love, she knows, is justified of love.

And I, I was a good child on the whole,
A meek and manageable child.   Why not?
I did not live, to have the faults of life :
There seemed more true life in my father's grave
Than in all England.   Since *that* threw me off
Who fain would cleave (his latest will, they say,
Consigned me to his land), I only thought
Of lying quiet there where I was thrown
Like sea-weed on the rocks, and suffering her   380
To prick me to a pattern with her pin,
Fibre from fibre, delicate leaf from leaf,

And dry out from my drowned anatomy
The last sea-salt left in me.
                                So it was.
I broke the copious curls upon my head
In braids, because she liked smooth-ordered hair.
I left off saying my sweet Tuscan words
Which still at any stirring of the heart
Came up to float across the English phrase
As lilies (*Bene* or *Che che*), because   390
She liked my father's child to speak his tongue.
I learnt the collects and the cathecism,
The creeds, from Athanasius back to Nice,
The Articles, the Tracts *against* the times
(By no means Buonaventure's "Prick of Love"),
And various popular synopses of
Inhuman doctrines never taught by John,
Because she liked instructed piety.
I learnt my complement of classic French
(Kept pure of Balzac and neologism)   400
And German also, since she liked a range
Of liberal education,— tongues, not books.
I learnt a little algebra, a little
Of the mathematics,— brushed with extreme flounce
The circle of the sciences, because
She misliked women who are frivolous.
I learnt the royal genealogies
Of Oviedo, the internal laws
Of the Burmese empire,— by how many feet
Mount Chimborazo outsoars Teneriffe.   410
What navigable river joins itself
To Lara, and what census of the year five
Was taken at Klagenfurt, — because she liked
A general insight into useful facts.
I learnt much music, — such as would have been

As quite impossible in Johnson's day
As still it might be wished — fine sleights of hand
And unimagined fingering, shuffling off
The hearer's soul through hurricanes of notes
To a noisy Tophet ; and I drew . . . costumes 420
From French engravings, nereids neatly draped
(With smirks of simmering godship) : I washed in
Landscapes from nature (rather say, washed out).
I danced the polka and Cellarius,
Spun glass, stuffed birds, and modelled flowers in wax,
Because she liked accomplishments in girls.
I read a score of books on womanhood
To prove, if women do not think at all,
They may teach thinking (to a maiden aunt
Or else the author), — books that boldly assert 430
Their right of comprehending husband's talk
When not too deep, and even of answering
With pretty "may it please you," or "so it is," —
Their rapid insight and fine aptitude,
Particular worth and general missionariness,
As long as they keep quiet by the fire
And never say "no" when the world says "ay,"
For that is fatal, — their angelic reach
Of virtue, chiefly used to sit and darn,
And fatten household sinners, — their, in brief, 440
Potential faculty in everything
Of abdicating power in it : she owned
She liked a woman to be womanly,
And English women, she thanked God and sighed
(Some people always sigh in thanking God)
Were models to the universe. And last
I learnt cross-stitch, because she did not like
To see me wear the night with empty hands
A-doing nothing. So, my shepherdess

Was something after all (the pastoral saints   450
Be praised for't), leaning lovelorn with pink eyes
To match her shoes, when I mistook the silks ;
Her head uncrushed by that round weight of hat
So strangely similar to the tortoise-shell
Which slew the tragic poet.

                              By the way,
The works of women are symbolical.
We sew, sew, prick our fingers, dull our sight,
Producing what ?   A pair of slippers, sir,
To put on when you're weary — or a stool
To stumble over and vex you . . . " curse that
      stool ! "   460
Or else at best, a cushion, where you lean
And sleep, and dream of something we are not
But would be for your sake.   Alas, alas !
This hurts most, this — that, after all, we are paid
The worth of our work, perhaps.

                              In looking down
Those years of education (to return)
I wonder if Brinvilliers suffered more
In the water-torture . . . flood succeeding flood
To drench the incapable throat and split the veins . . .
Than I did.   Certain of your feebler souls   470
Go out in such a process ; many pine
To a sick, inodorous light ; my own endured :
I had relations in the Unseen, and drew
The elemental nutriment and heat
From nature, as earth feels the sun at nights,
Or as a babe sucks surely in the dark.
I kept the life thrust on me, on the outside
Of the inner life with all its ample room
For heart and lungs, for will and intellect,
Inviolable by conventions.   God,   480

I thank thee for that grace of thine !
                                        At first
I felt no life which was not patience, — did
The thing she bade me, without heed to a thing
Beyond it, sat in just the chair she placed,
With back against the window, to exclude
The sight of the great lime-tree on the lawn,
Which seemed to have come on purpose from the
      woods
To bring the house a message, — ay, and walked
Demurely in her carpeted low rooms,
As if I should not, hearkening my own steps,   490
Misdoubt I was alive.   I read her books,
Was civil to her cousin, Romney Leigh,
Gave ear to her vicar, tea to her visitors,
And heard them whisper, when I changed a cup
(I blushed for joy at that), — " The Italian child,
For all her blue eyes and her quiet ways,
Thrives ill in England : she is paler yet
Than when we came the last time ; she will die."

" Will die."   My cousin, Romney Leigh, blushed
      too,
With sudden anger, and approaching me   500
Said low between his teeth, " You're wicked now ?
You wish to die and leave the world a-dusk
For others, with your naughty light blown out ?"
I looked into his face defyingly ;
He might have known that, being what I was,
'Twas natural to like to get away
As far as dead folk can : and then indeed
Some people make no trouble when they die.
He turned and went abruptly, slammed the door,
And shut his dog out.

                         Romney, Romney Leigh. 510
I have not named my cousin hitherto,
And yet I used him as a sort of friend ;
My elder by few years, but cold and shy
And absent . . . tender, when he thought of it,
Which scarcely was imperative, grave betimes,
As well as early master of Leigh Hall,
Whereof the nightmare sat upon his youth,
Repressing all its seasonable delights,
And agonising with a ghastly sense
Of universal hideous want and wrong   520
To incriminate possession.   When he came
From college to the country, very oft
He crossed the hill on visits to my aunt,
With gifts of blue grapes from the hothouses,
A book in one hand, — mere statistics (if
I chanced to lift the cover), count of all
The goats whose beards grow sprouting down toward
     hell
Against God's separative judgment-hour.
And she, she almost loved him, — even allowed
That sometimes he should seem to sigh my way ; 530
It made him easier to be pitiful,
And sighing was his gift.   So, undisturbed,
At whiles she let him shut my music up
And push my needles down, and lead me out
To see in that south angle of the house
The figs grow black as if by a Tuscan rock,
On some light pretext.   She would turn her head
At other moments, go to fetch a thing,
And leave me breath enough to speak with him,
For his sake ; it was simple.
                         Sometimes too   540
He would have saved me utterly, it seemed,

He stood and looked so.
                    Once, he stood so near,
He dropped a sudden hand upon my head
Bent down on woman's work, as soft as rain —
But then I rose and shook it off as fire,
The stranger's touch that took my father's place
Yet dared seem soft.
                I used him for a friend
Before I ever knew him for a friend.
'Twas better, 'twas worse also, afterward :
We came so close, we saw our differences   550
Too intimately.   Always Romney Leigh
Was looking for the worms, I for the gods.
A godlike nature his ; the gods look down,
Incurious of themselves ; and certainly
'Tis well I should remember, how, those days,
I was a worm too, and he looked on me.

A little by his act perhaps, yet more
By something in me, surely not my will,
I did not die.   But slowly, as one in swoon,
To whom life creeps back in the form of death,   560
With a sense of separation, a blind pain
Of blank obstruction, and a roar i' the ears
Of visionary chariots which retreat
As earth grows clearer . . . slowly, by degrees ;
I woke, rose up . . . where was I ? in the world ;
For uses therefore I must count worth while.

I had a little chamber in the house,
As green as any privet-hedge a bird
Might choose to build in, though the nest itself
Could show but dead-brown sticks and straws ; the
     walls   570

Were green, the carpet was pure green, the straight
Small bed was curtained greenly, and the folds
Hung green about the window which let in
The out-door world with all its greenery.
You could not push your head out and escape
A dash of dawn-dew from the honeysuckle,
But so you were baptized into the grace
And privilege of seeing. . . .

                      First, the lime
(I had enough there, of the lime, be sure, —
My morning-dream was often hummed away   580
By the bees in it) ; past the lime, the lawn,
Which, after sweeping broadly round the house,
Went trickling through the shrubberies in a stream
Of tender turf, and wore and lost itself
Among the acacias, over which you saw
The irregular line of elms by the deep lane
Which stopped the grounds and dammed the overflow
Of arbutus and laurel.   Out of sight
The lane was ; sunk so deep, no foreign tramp
Nor drover of wild ponies out of Wales   590
Could guess if lady's hall or tenant's lodge
Dispensed such odours, — though his stick well-crooked
Might reach the lowest trail of blossoming briar
Which dipped upon the wall.   Behind the elms,
And through their tops, you saw the folded hills
Striped up and down with hedges (burly oaks
Projecting from the line to show themselves),
Through which my cousin Romney's chimneys smoked
As still as when a silent mouth in frost
Breathes, showing where the woodlands hid Leigh
    Hall ;   600
While, far above, a jut of table-land,
A promontory without water, stretched, —

You could not catch it if the days were thick,
Or took it for a cloud ; but, otherwise,
The vigorous sun would catch it up at eve
And use it for an anvil till he had filled
The shelves of heaven with burning thunder-bolts,
Protesting against night and darkness : — then,
When all his setting trouble was resolved
To a trance of passive glory, you might see   610
In apparition on the golden sky
(Alas, my Giotto's background !) the sheep run
Along the fine clear outline, small as mice
That run along a witch's scarlet thread.

Not a grand nature.   Not my chestnut-woods
Of Vallombrosa, cleaving by the spurs
To the precipices.   Not my headlong leaps
Of waters, that cry out for joy or fear
In leaping through the palpitating pines,
Like a white soul tossed out to eternity   620
With thrills of time upon it.   Not indeed
My multitudinous mountains, sitting in
The magic circle, with the mutual touch
Electric, panting from their full deep hearts
Beneath the influent heavens, and waiting for
Communion and commission.   Italy
Is one thing, England one.
                         On English ground
You understand the letter, — ere the fall
How Adam lived in a garden.   All the fields
Are tied up fast with hedges, nosegay-like ;   630
The hills are crumpled plains, the plains parterres,
The trees, round, woolly, ready to be clipped,
And if you seek for any wilderness
You find, at best, a park.   A nature tamed

And grown domestic like a barn-door fowl,
Which does not awe you with its claws and beak,
Nor tempt you to an eyrie too high up,
But which, in cackling, sets you thinking of
Your eggs to-morrow at breakfast, in the pause
Of finer meditation.

            Rather say,   640
A sweet familiar nature, stealing in
As a dog might, or child, to touch your hand
Or pluck your gown, and humbly mind you so
Of presence and affection, excellent
For inner uses, from the things without.

I could not be unthankful, I who was
Entreated thus and holpen.   In the room
I speak of, ere the house was well awake,
And also after it was well asleep,
I sat alone, and drew the blessing in   650
Of all that nature.   With a gradual step,
A stir among the leaves, a breath, a ray,
It came in softly, while the angels made
A place for it beside me.   The moon came,
And swept my chamber clean of foolish thoughts.
The sun came, saying, " Shall I lift this light
Against the lime-tree, and you will not look ?
I make the birds sing — listen ! but, for you,
God never hears your voice, excepting when
You lie upon the bed at nights and weep."   660

Then, something moved me.   Then, I wakened up
More slowly than I verily write now,
But wholly, at last, I wakened, opened wide
The window and my soul, and let the airs
And out-door sights sweep gradual gospels in,

Regenerating what I was.   O, Life,
How oft we throw it off and think, — " Enough,
Enough of life in so much ! — here's a cause
For rupture ; — herein we must break with Life, 669
Or be ourselves unworthy ; here we are wronged,
Maimed, spoiled for aspiration : farewell, Life ! ''
And so, as froward babes, we hide our eyes
And think all ended. — Then, Life calls to us
In some transformed, apocalyptic voice,
Above us, or below us, or around :
Perhaps we name it Nature's voice, or Love's,
Tricking ourselves, because we are more ashamed
To own our compensations than our griefs :
Still, Life's voice ! — still, we make our peace with Life.

And I, so young then, was not sullen.   Soon   680
I used to get up early, just to sit
And watch the morning quicken in the gray,
And hear the silence open like a flower
Leaf after leaf, — and stroke with listless hand
The woodbine through the window, till at last
I came to do it with a sort of love,
At foolish unaware : whereat I smiled, —
A melancholy smile, to catch myself
Smiling for joy.
                          Capacity for joy   689
Admits temptation.   It seemed, next, worth while
To dodge the sharp sword set against my life ;
To slip down stairs through all the sleepy house,
As mute as any dream there, and escape
As a soul from the body, out of doors,
Glide through the shrubberies, drop into the lane,
And wander on the hills an hour or two,
Then back again before the house should stir.

Or else I sat on in my chamber green,
And lived my life, and thought my thoughts, and
    prayed
My prayers without the vicar ; read my books   700
Without considering whether they were fit
To do me good.   Mark, there.   We get no good
By being ungenerous, even to a book,
And calculating profits, — so much help
By so much reading.   It is rather when
We gloriously forget ourselves and plunge
Soul-forward, headlong, into a book's profound,
Impassioned for its beauty and salt of truth —
'Tis then we get the right good from a book.

I read much.   What my father taught before   710
From many a volume, Love re-emphasised
Upon the self-same pages : Theophrast
Grew tender with the memory of his eyes,
And Ælian made mine wet.   The trick of Greek
And Latin he had taught me, as he would
Have taught me wrestling or the game of fives
If such he had known, — most like a shipwrecked
    man
Who heaps his single platter with goats' cheese
And scarlet berries ; or like any man
Who loves but one, and so gives all at once,   720
Because he has it, rather than because
He counts it worthy.   Thus, my father gave ;
And thus, as did the women formerly
By young Achilles, when they pinned a veil
Across the boy's audacious front, and swept
With tuneful laughs the silver-fretted rocks,
He wrapt his little daughter in his large
Man's doublet, careless did it fit or no.

But, after I had read for memory,
I read for hope.   The path my father's foot   730
Had trod me out (which suddenly broke off
What time he dropped the wallet of the flesh
And passed), alone I carried on, and set
My child-heart 'gainst the thorny underwood,
To reach the grassy shelter of the trees.
Ah babe i' the wood, without a brother-babe !
My own self-pity, like the red-breast bird,
Flies back to cover all that past with leaves.

Sublimest danger, over which none weeps,
When any young wayfaring soul goes forth   740
Alone, unconscious of the perilous road,
The day-sun dazzling in his limpid eyes,
To thrust his own way, he an alien, through
The world of books !   Ah, you ! — you think it fine,
You clap hands — " A fair day ! " — you cheer him
    on,
As if the worst, could happen, were to rest
Too long beside a fountain.   Yet, behold,
Behold ! — the world of books is still the world,
And worldings in it are less merciful
And more puissant.   For the wicked there   750
Are winged like angels ; every knife that strikes
Is edged from elemental fire to assail
A spiritual life ; the beautiful seems right
By force of beauty, and the feeble wrong
Because of weakness ; power is justified
Though armed against Saint Michael ; many a crown
Covers bald foreheads.   In the book-world, true,
There's no lack, neither, of God's saints and kings,
That shake the ashes of the grave aside
From their calm locks and undiscomfited   760

Look steadfast truths against Time's changing mask.
True, many a prophet teaches in the roads ;
True, many a seer pulls down the flaming heavens
Upon his own head in strong martyrdom
In order to light men a moment's space.
But stay ! — who judges ? — who distinguishes
'Twixt Saul and Nahash justly, at first sight,
And leaves king Saul precisely at the sin,
To serve king David ? who discerns at once   769
The sound of the trumpets, when the trumpets blow
For Alaric as well as Charlemagne ?
Who judges wizards, and can tell true seers
From conjurers ? the child, there ?   Would you leave
That child to wander in a battle-field
And push his innocent smile against the guns ;
Or even in a catacomb, — his torch
Grown ragged in the fluttering air, and all
The dark a-mutter round him ? not a child.

I read books bad and good — some bad and good
At once (good aims not always make good books :
Well-tempered spades turn up ill-smelling soils   781
In digging vineyards even) ; books that prove
God's being so definitely, that man's doubt
Grows self-defined the other side the line,
Made atheist by suggestion ; moral books,
Exasperating to license ; genial books,
Discounting from the human dignity ;
And merry books, which set you weeping when
The sun shines, — ay, and melancholy books,
Which make you laugh that any one should weep 790
In this disjointed life for one wrong more.

The world of books is still the world, I write,
And both worlds have God's providence, thank God,

To keep and hearten : with some struggle, indeed,
Among the breakers, some hard swimming through
The deeps — I lost breath in my soul sometimes
And cried " God save me if there's any God,"
But, even so, God saved me ; and, being dashed
From error on to error, every turn
Still brought me nearer to the central truth.   800

I thought so.   All this anguish in the thick
Of men's opinions . . . press and counter-press,
Now up, now down, now underfoot, and now
Emergent . . . all the best of it, perhaps,
But throws you back upon a noble trust
And use of your own instinct, — merely proves
Pure reason stronger than bare inference
At strongest.   Try it, — fix against heaven's wall
The scaling-ladders of school logic — mount
Step by step ! — sight goes faster ; that still ray   810
Which strikes out from you, how, you cannot tell,
And why, you know not (did you eliminate,
That such as you indeed should analyse ?)
Goes straight and fast as light, and high as God.

The cygnet finds the water, but the man
Is born in ignorance of his element
And feels out blind at first, disorganised
By sin i' the blood,— his spirit-insight dulled
And crossed by his sensations.   Presently
He feels it quicken in the dark sometimes,   820
When, mark, be reverent, be obedient,
For such dumb motions of imperfect life
Are oracles of vital Deity
Attesting the Hereafter.   Let who says
" The soul's a clean white paper," rather say,

A palimpsest, a prophet's holograph
Defiled, erased and covered by a monk's, —
The apocalypse, by a Longus ! poring on
Which obscene text, we may discern perhaps
Some fair, fine trace of what was written once,   830
Some upstroke of an alpha and omega
Expressing the old scripture.

                              Books, books, books !
I had found the secret of a garret-room
Piled high with cases in my father's name,
Piled high, packed large,— where, creeping in and out
Among the giant fossils of my past,
Like some small nimble mouse between the ribs
Of a mastodon, I nibbled here and there
At this or that box, pulling through the gap,
In heats of terror, haste, victorious joy,   840
The first book first.   And how I felt it beat
Under my pillow, in the morning's dark,
An hour before the sun would let me read !
My books !   At last because the time was ripe,
I chanced upon the poets.

                              As the earth
Plunges in fury, when the internal fires
Have reached and pricked her heart, and, throwing
     flat
The marts and temples, the triumphal gates
And towers of observation, clears herself
To elemental freedom — thus, my soul,   850
At poetry's divine first finger-touch,
Let go conventions and sprang up surprised,
Convicted of the great eternities
Before two worlds.

                              What's this, Aurora Leigh,
You write so of the poets, and not laugh ?

Those virtuous liars, dreamers after dark,
Exaggerators of the sun and moon,
And soothsayers in a tea-cup ?
                                        I write so
Of the only truth-tellers now left to God,
The only speakers of essential truth,   860
Opposed to relative, comparative,
And temporal truths ; the only holders by
His sun-skirts, through conventional gray glooms ;
The only teachers who instruct mankind
From just a shadow on a charnel-wall
To find man's veritable stature out
Erect, sublime, — the measure of a man,
And that's the measure of an angel, says
The apostle.   Ay, and while your common men
Lay telegraphs, gauge railroads, reign, reap, dine,   870
And dust the flaunty carpets of the world
For kings to walk on, or our president,
The poet suddenly will catch them up
With his voice like a thunder, — " This is soul,
This is life, this word is being said in heaven,
Here's God down on us ! what are you about ? "
How all those workers start amid their work,
Look round, look up, and feel, a moment's space,
That carpet-dusting, though a pretty trade,
Is not the imperative labour after all.   880

My own best poets, am I one with you,
That thus I love you,— or but one through love ?
Does all this smell of thyme about my feet
Conclude my visit to your holy hill
In personal presence, or but testify
The rustling of your vesture through my dreams
With influent odours ?   When my joy and pain,

My thought and aspiration like the stops
Of pipe or flute, are absolutely dumb
Unless melodious, do you play on me   890
My pipers,— and if, sooth, you did not blow,
Would no sound come ? or is the music mine,
As a man's voice or breath is called his own,
Inbreathed by the Life-breather ?   There's a doubt
For cloudy seasons !
                                But the sun was high
When first I felt my pulses set themselves
For concord ; when the rhythmic turbulence
Of blood and brain swept outward upon words,
As wind upon the alders, blanching them
By turning up their under-natures till   900
They trembled in dilation.   O delight
And triumph of the poet, who would say
A man's mere " yes," a woman's common " no,"
A little human hope of that or this,
And says the word so that it burns you through
With a special revelation, shakes the heart
Of all the men and women in the world,
As if one came back from the dead and spoke,
With eyes too happy, a familiar thing
Become divine i' the utterance ! while for him   910
The poet, speaker, he expands with joy ;
The palpitating angel in his flesh
Thrills inly with consenting fellowship
To those innumerous spirits who sun themselves
Outside of time.
                        O life, O poetry,
— Which means life in life ! cognisant of life
Beyond this blood-beat, passionate for truth
Beyond these senses ! — poetry, my life,
My eagle, with both grappling feet still hot

From Zeus's thunder, who hast ravished me   920
Away from all the shepherds, sheep, and dogs,
And set me in the Olympian roar and round
Of luminous faces for a cup-bearer,
To keep the mouths of all the godheads moist
For everlasting laughters, — I myself
Half drunk across the beaker with their eyes !
How those gods look !
           Enough so, Ganymede,
We shall not bear above a round or two.
We drop the golden cup at Heré's foot
And swoon back to the earth, — and find ourselves 930
Face-down among the pine-cones, cold with dew,
While the dogs bark, and many a shepherd scoffs,
" What's come now to the youth ? "   Such ups and
    downs
Have poets.
        Am I such indeed ?   The name
Is royal, and to sign it like a queen
Is what I dare not, — though some royal blood
Would seem to tingle in me now and then,
With sense of power and ache, — with imposthumes
And manias usual to the race.   Howbeit
I dare not : 'tis too easy to go mad   940
And ape a Bourbon in a crown of straws ;
The thing's too common.
          Many fervent souls
Strike rhyme on rhyme, who would strike steel on
    steel
If steel had offered, in a restless heat
Of doing something.   Many tender souls
Have strung their losses on a rhyming thread,
As children cowslips : — the more pains they take,
The work more withers.   Young men, ay, and maids,

Too often sow their wild oats in tame verse,
Before they sit down under their own vine   950
And live for use.   Alas, near all the birds
Will sing at dawn, — and yet we do not take
The chaffering swallow for the holy lark.
In those days, though, I never analysed,
Not even myself.   Analysis comes late.
You catch a sight of Nature, earliest,
In full front sun-face, and your eyelids wink
And drop before the wonder of 't ; you miss
The form, through seeing the light.   I lived, those
        days,
And wrote because I lived — unlicensed else ;   960
My heart beat in my brain.   Life's violent flood
Abolished bounds, — and, which my neighbour's field,
Which mine, what mattered ? it is thus in youth !
We play at leap-frog over the god Term ;
The love within us and the love without
Are mixed, confounded ; if we are loved or love,
We scarce distinguish : thus, with other power ;
Being acted on and acting seem the same :
In that first onrush of life's chariot-wheels,
We know not if the forests move or we.   970

And so, like most young poets, in a flush
Of individual life I poured myself
Along the veins of others, and achieved
Mere lifeless imitations of live verse,
And made the living answer for the dead,
Profaning nature.   " Touch not, do not taste,
Nor handle," — we're too legal, who write young :
We beat the phorminx till we hurt our thumbs,
As if still ignorant of counterpoint ;   979
We call the Muse, — " O Muse, benignant Muse," —

As if we had seen her purple-braided head,
With the eyes in it, start between the boughs
As often as a stag's.   What make-believe,
With so much earnest ! what effete results
From virile efforts ! what cold wire-drawn odes
From such white heats ! — bucolics, where the cows
Would scare the writer if they splashed the mud
In lashing off the flies, — didactics, driven
Against the heels of what the master said ;
And counterfeiting epics, shrill with trumps   990
A babe might blow between two straining cheeks
Of bubbled rose, to make his mother laugh ;
And elegiac griefs, and songs of love,
Like cast-off nosegays picked up on the road,
The worse for being warm : all these things, writ
On happy mornings, with a morning heart,
That leaps for love, is active for resolve,
Weak for art only.   Oft, the ancient forms
Will thrill, indeed, in carrying the young blood.
The wine-skins, now and then, a little warped, 1000
Will crack even, as the new wine gurgles in.
Spare the old bottles ! — spill not the new wine.

By Keats's soul, the man who never stepped
In gradual progress like another man,
But, turning grandly on his central self,
Ensphered himself in twenty perfect years
And died, not young (the life of a long life
Distilled to a mere drop, falling like a tear
Upon the world's cold cheek to make it burn
For ever) ; by that strong excepted soul,   1010
I count it strange and hard to understand
That nearly all young poets should write old,
That Pope was sexagenary at sixteen,

And beardless Byron academical,
And so with others.   It may be perhaps
Such have not settled long and deep enough
In trance, to attain to clairvoyance, — and still
The memory mixes with the vision, spoils,
And works it turbid.

                Or perhaps, again,
In order to discover the Muse-Sphinx,   1020
The melancholy desert must sweep round,
Behind you as before. —

                For me, I wrote
False poems, like the rest, and thought them true
Because myself was true in writing them.
I peradventure have writ true ones since
With less complacence.

                But I could not hide
My quickening inner life from those at watch.
They saw a light at a window, now and then,
They had not set there : who had set it there ?
My father's sister started when she caught   1030
My soul agaze in my eyes.   She could not say
I had no business with a sort of soul,
But plainly she objected, — and demurred
That souls were dangerous things to carry straight
Through all the spilt saltpetre of the world.
She said sometimes " Aurora, have you done
Your task this morning ? have you read that book ?
And are you ready for the crochet here ? " —
As if she said " I know there's something wrong ;
I know I have not ground you down enough   1040
To flatten and bake you to a wholesome crust
For household uses and proprieties,
Before the rain has got into my barn
And set the grains a-sprouting.   What, you're green

With out-door impudence ? you almost grow ? "
To which I answered, " Would she hear my task,
And verify my abstract of the book ?
Or should I sit down to the crochet work ?
Was such her pleasure ?"   Then I sat and teased
The patient needle till it split the thread,   1050
Which oozed off from it in meandering lace
From hour to hour.   I was not, therefore, sad ;
My soul was singing at a work apart
Behind the wall of sense, as safe from harm
As sings the lark when sucked up out of sight
In vortices of glory and blue air.

And so, through forced work and spontaneous work,
The inner life informed the outer life,
Reduced the irregular blood to a settled rhythm, 1059
Made cool the forehead with fresh-sprinkling dreams,
And, rounding to the spheric soul the thin,
Pined body, struck a colour up the cheeks
Though somewhat faint.   I clenched my brows across
My blue eyes greatening in the looking-glass,
And said " We'll live, Aurora ! we'll be strong.
The dogs are on us — but we will not die."

Whoever lives true life will love true love.
I learnt to love that England.   Very oft,
Before the day was born, or otherwise
Through secret windings of the afternoons,   1070
I threw my hunters off and plunged myself
Among the deep hills, as a hunted stag
Will take the waters, shivering with the fear
And passion of the course.   And when at last
Escaped, so many a green slope built on slope
Betwixt me and the enemy's house behind,

I darea to rest, or wander, in a rest
Made sweeter for the step upon the grass,
And view the ground's most gentle dimplement
(As if God's finger touched but did not press   1080
In making England), such an up and down
Of verdure, — nothing too much up or down,
A ripple of land ; such little hills, the sky
Can stoop to tenderly and the wheatfields climb ;
Such nooks of valleys lined with orchises,
Fed full of noises by invisible streams ;
And open pastures where you scarcely tell
White daisies from white dew, — at intervals
The mythic oaks and elm-trees standing out
Self-poised upon their prodigy of shade, —   1090
I thought my father's land was worthy too
Of being my Shakespeare's.

                Very oft alone,
Unlicensed ; not unfrequently with leave
To walk the third with Romney and his friend
The rising painter, Vincent Carrington,
Whom men judge hardly as bee-bonneted,
Because he holds that, paint a body well,
You paint a soul by implication, like
The grand first Master.   Pleasant walks ! for if
He said " When I was last in Italy,"   1100
It sounded as an instrument that's played
Too far off for the tune — and yet it's fine
To listen.

        Often we walked only two
If cousin Romney pleased to walk with me.
We read, or talked, or quarrelled, as it chanced.
We were not lovers, nor even friends well-matched :
Say rather, scholars upon different tracks,
And thinkers disagreed : he, overfull

Of what is, and I, haply, overbold   1109
For what might be.
                        But then the thrushes sang,
And shook my pulses and the elms' new leaves :
At which I turned, and held my finger up,
And bade him mark that, howsoe'er the world
Went ill, as he related, certainly
The thrushes still sang in it.   At the word
His brow would soften, — and he bore with me
In melancholy patience, not unkind,
While breaking into voluble ecstasy
I flattered all the beauteous country round,
As poets use, the skies, the clouds, the fields,   1120
The happy violets hiding from the roads
The primroses run down to, carrying gold ;
The tangled hedgerows, where the cows push out
Impatient horns and tolerant churning mouths
'Twixt dripping ash-boughs, — hedgerows all alive
With birds and gnats and large white butterflies
Which look as if the May-flower had caught life
And palpitated forth upon the wind ;
Hills, vales, woods, netted in a silver mist,
Farms, granges, doubled up among the hills ;   1130
And cattle grazing in the watered vales,
And cottage-chimneys smoking from the woods,
And cottage-gardens smelling everywhere,
Confused with smell of orchards.   "See," I said,
" And see ! is God not with us on the earth ?
And shall we put Him down by aught we do ?
Who says there's nothing for the poor and vile
Save poverty and wickedness ? behold ! "
And ankle-deep in English grass I leaped
And clapped my hands, and called all very fair.   1140

In the beginning when God called all good,
Even then was evil near us, it is writ ;
But we indeed who call things good and fair,
The evil is upon us while we speak ;
Deliver us from evil, let us pray.

SECOND BOOK

TIMES followed one another.   Came a morn
I stood upon the brink of twenty years,
And looked before and after, as I stood
Woman and artist, — either incomplete,
Both credulous of completion.   There I held
The whole creation in my little cup,
And smiled with thirsty lips before I drank
" Good health to you and me, sweet neighbour mine,
And all these peoples."

                      I was glad, that day ;
The June was in me, with its multitudes   10
Of nightingales all singing in the dark,
And rosebuds reddening where the calyx split.
I felt so young, so strong, so sure of God !
So glad, I could not choose be very wise !
And, old at twenty, was inclined to pull
My childhood backward in a childish jest
To see the face of 't once more, and farewell !
In which fantastic mood I bounded forth
At early morning, — would not wait so long
As even to snatch my bonnet by the strings,   20
But, brushing a green trail across the lawn
With my gown in the dew, took will and away
Among the acacias of the shrubberies,
To fly my fancies in the open air

And keep my birthday, till my aunt awoke
To stop good dreams.   Meanwhile I murmured on
As honeyed bees keep humming to themselves,
" The worthiest poets have remained uncrowned
Till death has bleached their foreheads to the bone ;
And so with me it must be unless I prove   30
Unworthy of the grand adversity,
And certainly I would not fail so much.
What, therefore, if I crown myself to-day
In sport, not pride, to learn the feel of it,
Before my brows be numbed as Dante's own
To all the tender pricking of such leaves ?
Such leaves ! what leaves ? "
                                I pulled the branches down
To choose from.
                    " Not the bay ! I choose no bay
(The fates deny us if we are overbold),
Nor myrtle — which means chiefly love ; and love 40
Is something awful which one dares not touch
So early o' mornings.   This verbena strains
The point of passionate fragrance ; and hard by,
This guelder-rose, at far too slight a beck
Of the wind, will toss about her flower-apples.
Ah — there's my choice, — that ivy on the wall,
That headlong ivy ! not a leaf will grow
But thinking of a wreath.   Large leaves, smooth leaves,
Serrated like my vines, and half as green.
I like such ivy, bold to leap a height   50
'Twas strong to climb ; as good to grow on graves
As twist about a thyrsus ; pretty too
(And that's not ill) when twisted round a comb."
Thus speaking to myself, half singing it,
Because some thoughts are fashioned like a bell
To ring with once being touched, I drew a wreath

Drenched, blinding me with dew, across my brow,
And fastening it behind so, turning faced
 . . .   My public ! — cousin Romney — with a
       mouth
Twice graver than his eyes.
                                    I stood there fixed, — 60
My arms up, like the caryatid, sole
Of some abolished temple, helplessly
Persistent in a gesture which derides
A former purpose.   Yet my blush was flame,
As if from flax, not stone.
                                    " Aurora Leigh,
The earliest of Auroras ! "
                                    Hand stretched out
I clasped, as shipwrecked men will clasp a hand,
Indifferent to the sort of palm.   The tide
Had caught me at my pastime, writing down
My foolish name too near upon the sea   70
Which drowned me with a blush as foolish.   " You,
My cousin ! "
                                    The smile died out in his eyes
And dropped upon his lips, a cold dead weight,
For just a moment, " Here's a book I found !
No name writ on it — poems, by the form ;
Some Greek upon the margin, — lady's Greek
Without the accents.   Read it ?   Not a word.
I saw at once the thing had witchcraft in't,
Whereof the reading calls up dangerous spirits :
I rather bring it to the witch."
                                    " My book.   80
You found it " . . .
                                    " In the hollow by the stream
That beech leans down into — of which you said
The Oread in it has a Naiad's heart

And pines for waters."
                    " Thank you."
                                " Thanks to *you*
My cousin ! that I have seen you not too much
Witch, scholar, poet, dreamer, and the rest,
To be a woman also."
                    With a glance
The smile rose in his eyes again and touched
The ivy on my forehead, light as air.
I answered gravely " Poets needs must be   90
Or men or women — more's the pity."
                                " Ah,
But men, and still less women, happily,
Scarce need be poets.   Keep to the green wreath,
Since even dreaming of the stone and bronze
Brings headaches, pretty cousin, and defiles
The clean white morning dresses."
                            " So you judge !
Because I love the beautiful I must
Love pleasure chiefly, and be overcharged
For ease and whiteness ! well, you know the world,
And only miss your cousin, 'tis not much.   100
But learn this ; I would rather take my part
With God's Dead, who afford to walk in white
Yet spread His glory, than keep quiet here
And gather up my feet from even a step
For fear to soil my gown in so much dust.
I choose to walk at all risks. — Here, if heads
That hold a rhythmic thought, much ache perforce,
For my part I choose headaches, — and to-day's
My birthday."
            " Dear Aurora, choose instead   109
To cure them.   You have balsams."
                            " I perceive.

The headache is too noble for my sex.
You think the heartache would sound decenter,
Since that's the woman's special, proper ache,
And altogether tolerable, except
To a woman.''
                          Saying which, I loosed my wreath,
And swinging it beside me as I walked,
Half-petulant, half-playful, as we walked,
I sent a sidelong look to find his thought, —
As falcon set on falconer's finger may,
With sidelong head, and startled, braving eye,   120
Which means, ''You'll see — you'll see ! I'll soon
      take flight,
You shall not hinder.''   He, as shaking out
His hand and answering ''Fly then,'' did not speak,
Except by such a gesture.   Silently
We paced, until, just coming into sight
Of the house-windows, he abruptly caught
At one end of the swinging wreath, and said
'' Aurora !'' There I stopped short, breath and all.

'' Aurora, let's be serious, and throw by   129
This game of head and heart.   Life means, be sure,
Both heart and head, — both active, both complete,
And both in earnest.   Men and women make
The world, as head and heart make human life.
Work man, work woman, since there's work to do
In this beleaguered earth, for head and heart,
And thought can never do the work of love :
But work for ends, I mean for uses, not
For such sleek fringes (do you call them ends,
Still less God's glory ?) as we sew ourselves
Upon the velvet of those baldaquins   140
Held 'twixt us and the sun.   That book of yours,

I have not read a page of; but I toss
A rose up — it falls calyx down, you see !
The chances are that, being a woman, young
And pure, with such a pair of large, calm eyes,
You write as well . . . and ill . . . upon
    the whole,
As other women. If as well, what then?
If even a little better, . . . still, what then?
We want the Best in art now, or no art.
The time is done for facile settings up   150
Of minnow gods, nymphs here and tritons there ;
The polytheists have gone out in God,
That unity of Bests. No bests, no God !
And so with art, we say. Give art's divine,
Direct, indubitable, real as grief,
Or leave us to the grief we grow ourselves
Divine by overcoming with mere hope
And most prosaic patience. You, you are young
As Eve with nature's daybreak on her face,   159
But this same world you are come to, dearest coz,
Has done with keeping birthdays, saves her wreaths
To hang upon her ruins, — and forgets
To rhyme the cry with which she still beats back
Those savage, hungry dogs that hunt her down
To the empty grave of Christ. The world's hard
    pressed :
The sweat of labour in the early curse
Has (turning acrid in six thousand years)
Become the sweat of torture. Who has time,
An hour's time . . . think ! — to sit upon a
    bank
And hear the cymbal tinkle in white hands ?   170
When Egypt's slain, I say, let Miriam sing ! —
Before — where's Moses ? ''

                  " Ah, exactly that.
Where's Moses ? — is a Moses to be found ?
You'll seek him vainly in the bulrushes,
While I in vain touch cymbals. Yet concede,
Such sounding brass has done some actual good
(The application in a woman's hand,
If that were credible, being scarcely spoilt,)
In colonising beehives."

                  " There it is ! —
You play beside a death-bed like a child,   180
Yet measure to yourself a prophet's place
To teach the living. None of all these things
Can women understand. You generalise
Oh, nothing, — not even grief ! Your quick-breathed
     hearts,
So sympathetic to the personal pang,
Close on each separate knife-stroke, yielding up
A whole life at each wound, incapable
Of deepening, widening a large lap of life
To hold the world-full woe. The human race
To you means, such a child, or such a man,   190
You saw one morning waiting in the cold,
Beside that gate, perhaps. You gather up
A few such cases, and when strong sometimes
Will write of factories and of slaves, as if
Your father were a negro, and your son
A spinner in the mills. All's yours and you,
All, coloured with your blood, or otherwise
Just nothing to you. Why, I call you hard
To general suffering. Here's the world half-blind
With intellectual light, half-brutalised   200
With civilisation, having caught the plague
In silks from Tarsus, shrieking east and west
Along a thousand railroads, mad with pain

And sin too !   .   .   .   does one woman of you all
(You who weep easily) grow pale to see
This tiger shake his cage ? — does one of you
Stand still from dancing, stop from stringing pearls,
And pine and die because of the great sum
Of universal anguish ? — Show me a tear
Wet as Cordelia's, in eyes bright as yours,   210
Because the world is mad.   You cannot count,
That you should weep for this account, not you !
You weep for what you know.   A red-haired child
Sick in a fever, if you touch him once,
Though but so little as with a finger-tip,
Will set you weeping ; but a million sick   .   .   .
You could as soon weep for the rule of three
Or compound fractions.   Therefore, this same world,
Uncomprehended by you, must remain
Uninfluenced by you. — Women as you are,   220
Mere women, personal and passionate,
You give us doating mothers, and perfect wives,
Sublime Madonnas, and enduring saints !
We get no Christ from you, — and verily
We shall not get a poet, in my mind."
" With which conclusion you conclude ! "   .   .   .
                                        " But this,"
That you, Aurora, with the large live brow
And steady eyelids, cannot condescend
To play at art, as children play at swords,
To show a pretty spirit, chiefly admired   230
Because true action is impossible.
You never can be satisfied with praise
Which men give women when they judge a book
Not as mere work but as mere woman's work,
Expressing the comparative respect
Which means the absolute scorn.   " Oh, excellent,

" What grace, what facile turns, what fluent sweeps,
" What delicate discernment . . . almost thought !
" The book does honour to the sex, we hold.
" Among our female authors we make room   240
" For this fair writer, and congratulate
" The country that produces in these times
" Such women, competent to   .   .   .   spell."

          " Stop there,"
I answered, burning through his thread of talk
With a quick flame of emotion, — " You have read
My soul, if not my book, and argue well
I would not condescend   .   .   .   we will nct say
To such a kind of praise (a worthless end
Is praise of all kinds), but to such a use
Of holy art and golden life.   I am young,   250
And peradventure weak — you tell me so —
Through being a woman.   And, for all the rest,
Take thanks for justice.   I would rather dance
At fairs on tight-rope, till the babies dropped
Their gingerbread for joy, — than shift the types
For tolerable verse, intolerable
To men who act and suffer.   Better far
Pursue a frivolous trade by serious means,
Than a sublime art frivolously."

         " You,
Choose nobler work than either, O moist eyes   260
And hurrying lips and heaving heart !   We are young,
Aurora, you and I.   The world, — look round, —
The world, we're come to late, is swollen hard
With perished generations and their sins :
The civiliser's spade grinds horribly
On dead men's bones, and cannot turn up soil
That's otherwise than fetid.   All success
Proves partial failure ; all advance implies   268

What's left behind ; all triumph, something crushed
At the chariot-wheels ; all government, some wrong
And rich men make the poor, who curse the rich,
Who agonise together, rich and poor,
Under and over, in the social spasm
And crisis of the ages.   Here's an age
That makes its own vocation ! here we have stepped
Across the bounds of time ! here's nought to see,
But just the rich man and just Lazarus,
And both in torments, with a mediate gulf,
Though not a hint of Abraham's bosom.   Who
Being man, Aurora, can stand calmly by   280
And view these things, and never tease his soul
For some great cure ?   No physic for this grief,
In all the earth and heavens too ? "

                              " You believe
In God, for your part ? — ay ? that He who makes
Can make good things from ill things, best from worst,
As men plant tulips upon dunghills when
They wish them finest ? "

                              " True.   A death-heat is
The same as life-heat, to be accurate,
And in all nature is no death at all,
As men account of death, so long as God   290
Stands witnessing for life perpetually,
By being just God.   That's abstract truth, I know,
Philosophy, or sympathy with God :
But I, I sympathise with man, not God
(I think I was a man for chiefly this),
And when I stand beside a dying bed,
'Tis death to me.   Observe, — it had not much
Consoled the race of mastodons to know,
Before they went to fossil, that anon
Their place would quicken with the elephant.   300

They were not elephants but mastodons ;
And I, a man, as men are now and not
As men may be hereafter, feel with men
In the agonising present.''
       `` Is it so,''
I said, `` my cousin ? is the world so bad,
While I hear nothing of it through the trees ?
The world was always evil, — but so bad ? ''

`` So bad, Aurora. Dear, my soul is grey
With poring over the long sum of ill ;
So much for vice, so much for discontent,   310
So much for the necessities of power,
So much for the connivances of fear,
Coherent in statistical despairs
With such a total of distracted life, . . .
To see it down in figures on a page,
Plain, silent, clear, as God sees through the earth
The sense of all the graves, — that's terrible
For one who is not God, and cannot right
The wrong he looks on. May I choose indeed,
But vow away my years, my means, my aims,   320
Among the helpers, if there's any help
In such a social strait ? The common blood
That swings along my veins is strong enough
To draw me to this duty.''
        Then I spoke.
`` I have not stood long on the strand of life,
And these salt waters have had scarcely time
To creep so high up as to wet my feet :
I cannot judge these tides — I shall, perhaps.
A woman's always younger than a man
At equal years, because she is disallowed   330
Maturing by the outdoor sun and air,

And kept in long-clothes past the age to walk.
Ah well, I know you men judge otherwise !
You think a woman ripens, as a peach,
In the cheeks chiefly.   Pass it to me now ;
I'm young in age, and younger still, I think,
As a woman.   But a child may say amen
To a bishop's prayer and feel the way it goes,
And I, incapable to loose the knot
Of social questions, can approve, applaud   340
August compassion, Christian thoughts that shoot
Beyond the vulgar white of personal aims.
Accept my reverence."
                              There he glowed on me
With all his face and eyes.   " No other help ? "
Said he — " no more than so ? "
                              " What help ? " I asked.
" You'd scorn my help, — as Nature's self, you say,
Has scorned to put her music in my mouth
Because a woman's.   Do you now turn round
And ask for what a woman cannot give ? "

" For what she only can, I turn and ask,"   350
He answered, catching up my hands in his,
And dropping on me from his high-eaved brow
The full weight of his soul, — " I ask for love,
And that, she can ; for life in fellowship
Through bitter duties — that, I know she can ;
For wifehood — will she ? "
                              " Now," I said, " may God
Be witness 'twixt us two ! " and with the word,
Meseemed I floated into a sudden light
Above his stature, — " am I proved too weak
To stand alone, yet strong enough to bear   360
Such leaners on my shoulder ? poor to think,

Yet rich enough to sympathise with thought ?
Incompetent to sing, as blackbirds can,
Yet competent to love, like HIM ? "

　　　　　　　　I paused ;
Perhaps I darkened, as the lighthouse will
That turns upon the sea.　　" It's always so.
Anything does for a wife."

　　　　　　　" Aurora, dear,
And dearly honoured," — he pressed in at once
With eager utterance, — " you translate me ill.
I do not contradict my thought of you　　　　　370
Which is most reverent, with another thought
Found less so.　If your sex is weak for art
(And I, who said so, did but honour you
By using truth in courtship), it is strong
For life and duty.　Place your fecund heart
In mine, and let us blossom for the world
That wants love's colour in the grey of time.
My talk, meanwhile, is arid to you, ay,
Since all my talk can only set you where
You look down coldly on the arena-heaps　　　380
Of headless bodies, shapeless, indistinct !
The Judgment-Angel scarce would find his way
Through such a heap of generalised distress
To the individual man with lips and eyes,
Much less Aurora.　Ah, my sweet, come down,
And hand in hand we'll go where yours shall touch
These victims, one by one ! till, one by one,
The formless, nameless trunk of every man
Shall seem to wear a head with hair you know,
And every woman catch your mother's face　　　390
To melt you into passion."

　　　　　　　" I am a girl,"
I answered slowly ; " you do well to name

My mother's face.   Though far too early, alas,
God's hand did interpose 'twixt it and me,
I know so much of love as used to shine
In that face and another.   Just so much ;
No more indeed at all.   I have not seen
So much love since, I pray you pardon me,
As answers even to make a marriage with
In this cold land of England.   What you love   40c
Is not a woman, Romney, but a cause :
You want a helpmate, not a mistress, sir,
A wife to help your ends, — in her no end.
Your cause is noble, your ends excellent,
But I, being most unworthy of these and that,
Do otherwise conceive of love.   Farewell."

"Farewell, Aurora ? you reject me thus ?"
He said.
            "Sir, you were married long ago.
You have a wife already whom you love,
Your social theory.   Bless you both, I say.   410
For my part, I am scarcely meek enough
To be the handmaid of a lawful spouse.
Do I look a Hagar, think you ?"
                              "So you jest."

"Nay, so, I speak in earnest," I replied.
"You treat of marriage too much like, at least,
A chief apostle : you would bear with you
A wife . . . a sister . . . shall we speak it out ?
A sister of charity."
                  "Then, must it be
Indeed farewell ?   And was I so far wrong
In hope and in illusion, when I took   420
The woman to be nobler than the man,

Yourself the noblest woman, in the use
And comprehension of what love is, — love,
That generates the likeness of itself
Through all heroic duties ?. so far wrong,
In saying bluntly, venturing truth on love,
' Come, human creature, love and work with me,' —
Instead of ' Lady, thou art wondrous fair,
' And, where the Graces walk before, the Muse
' Will follow at the lightning of their eyes,   430
' And where the Muse walks, lovers need to creep :
' Turn round and love me, or I die of love.' ''

With quiet indignation I broke in.
" You misconceive the question like a man,
Who sees a woman as the complement
Of his sex merely.   You forget too much
That every creature, female as the male,
Stands single in responsible act and thought
As also in birth and death.   Whoever says
To a loyal woman, ' Love and work with me,'   440
Will get fair answers if the work and love,
Being good themselves, are good for her — the best
She was born for.   Women of a softer mood,
Surprised by men when scarcely awake to life,
Will sometimes only hear the first word, love,
And catch up with it any kind of work,
Indifferent, so that dear love go with it.
I do not blame such women, though, for love,
They pick much oakum ; earth's fanatics make   449
Too frequently heaven's saints.   But *me* your work
Is not the best for, — nor your love the best,
Nor able to commend the kind of work
For love's sake merely.   Ah, you force me, sir,
To be overbold in speaking of myself :

I too have my vocation, — work to do,
The heavens and earth have set me since I changed
My father's face for theirs, and, though your world
Were twice as wretched as you represent,
Most serious work, most necessary work
As any of the economists'.   Reform,   460
Make trade a Christian possibility,
And individual right no general wrong ;
Wipe out earth's furrows of the Thine and Mine,
And leave one green for men to play at bowls,
With innings for them all ! . . .   What then, indeed,
If mortals are not greater by the head
Than any of their prosperities ? what then,
Unless the artist keep up open roads
Betwixt the seen and unseen, — bursting through
The best of your conventions with his best,   470
The speakable, imaginable best
God bids him speak, to prove what lies beyond
Both speech and imagination ?   A starved man
Exceeds a fat beast : we'll not barter, sir,
The beautiful for barley. — And, even so,
I hold you will not compass your poor ends
Of barley-feeding and material ease,
Without a poet's individualism
To work your universal.   It takes a soul,
To move a body : it takes a high-souled man,   480
To move the masses, even to a cleaner stye :
It takes the ideal, to blow a hair's-breadth off
The dust of the actual. — Ah, your Fouriers failed,
Because not poets enough to understand
That life develops from within. —— For me,
Perhaps I am not worthy, as you say,
Of work like this : perhaps a woman's soul
Aspires, and not creates : yet we aspire,

And yet I'll try out your perhapses, sir,
And if I fail . . . why, burn me up my straw   490
Like other false works — I'll not ask for grace ;
Your scorn is better, cousin Romney.   I
Who love my art, would never wish it lower
To suit my stature.   I may love my art.
You'll grant that even a woman may love art,
Seeing that to waste true love on anything
Is womanly, past question.''
                                        I retain
The very last word which I said that day,
As you the creaking of the door, years past,
Which let upon you such disabling news   500
You ever after have been graver.   He,
His eyes, the motions in his silent mouth,
Were fiery points on which my words were caught,
Transfixed for ever in my memory
For his sake, not their own.   And yet I know
I did not love him . . . nor he me . . . that's
          sure . . .
And what I said is unrepented of,
As truth is always.   Yet . . . a princely man ! —
If hard to me, heroic for himself !
He bears down on me through the slanting years, 510
The stronger for the distance.   If he had loved,
Ay, loved me, with that retributive face, . . .
I might have been a common woman now
And happier, less known and less left alone,
Perhaps a better woman after all,
With chubby children hanging on my neck
To keep me low and wise.   Ah me, the vines
That bear such fruit are proud to stoop with it.
The palm stands upright in a realm of sand.

And I, who spoke the truth then, stand upright, 520
Still worthy of having spoken out the truth,
By being content I spoke it though it set
Him there, me here. — O woman's vile remorse,
To hanker after a mere name, a show,
A supposition, a potential love !
Does every man who names love in our lives
Become a power for that ? is love's true thing
So much best to us, that what personates love
Is next best ?   A potential love, forsooth !
I'm not so vile.   No, no — he cleaves, I think, 530
This man, this image, — chiefly for the wrong
And shock he gave my life, in finding me
Precisely where the devil of my youth
Had set me, on those mountain-peaks of hope
All glittering with the dawn-dew, all erect
And famished for the noon, — exclaiming, while
I looked for empire and much tribute, " Come,
I have some worthy work for thee below.
Come, sweep my barns and keep my hospitals,
And I will pay thee with a current coin   540
Which men give women."

                As we spoke, the grass
Was trod in haste beside us, and my aunt,
With smile distorted by the sun, — face, voice
As much at issue with the summer-day
As if you brought a candle out of doors,
Broke in with " Romney, here ! — My child, entreat
Your cousin to the house, and have your talk,
If girls must talk upon their birthdays.   Come."

He answered for me calmly, with pale lips
That seemed to motion for a smile in vain,   550
" The talk is ended, madam, where we stand.

Your brother's daughter has dismissed me here ;
And all my answer can be better said
Beneath the trees, than wrong by such a word
Your house's hospitalities.   Farewell.''

With that he vanished.   I could hear his heel
Ring bluntly in the lane, as down he leapt
The short way from us. — Then a measured speech
Withdrew me.   '' What means this, Aurora Leigh ?
My brother's daughter has dismissed my guests ? ''

The lion in me felt the keeper's voice   561
Through all its quivering dewlaps ; I was quelled
Before her, — meekened to the child she knew :
I prayed her pardon, said '' I had little thought
To give dismissal to a guest of hers,
In letting go a friend of mine who came
To take me into service as a wife, —
No more than that, indeed.''

                '' No more, no more ?
Pray Heaven,'' she answered, '' that I was not mad.
I could not mean to tell her to her face   570
That Romney Leigh had asked me for a wife,
And I refused him ? ''

                '' Did he ask ? '' I said ;
'' I think he rather stooped to take me up
For certain uses which he found to do
For something called a wife.   He never asked.''

'' What stuff ! '' she answered ; '' are they queens,
    these girls ?
They must have mantles, stitched with twenty silks,
Spread out upon the ground, before they'll step
One footstep for the noblest lover born.''

"But I am born," I said with firmness, "I,   580
To walk another way than his, dear aunt."

"You walk, you walk!   A babe at thirteen months
Will walk as well as you," she cried in haste,
"Without a steadying finger.   Why, you child,
God help you, you are groping in the dark,
For all this sunlight.   You suppose, perhaps,
That you, sole offspring of an opulent man,
Are rich and free to choose a way to walk?
You think, and it's a reasonable thought,
That I, beside, being well to do in life,   590
Will leave my handful in my niece's hand
When death shall paralyse these fingers?   Pray,
Pray, child, albeit I know you love me not,
As if you loved me, that I may not die!
For when I die and leave you, out you go
(Unless I make room for you in my grave),
Unhoused, unfed, my dear poor brother's lamb
(Ah heaven! — that pains!) — without a right to
       crop
A single blade of grass beneath these trees,
Or cast a lamb's small shadow on the lawn,   600
Unfed, unfolded!   Ah, my brother, here's
The fruit you planted in your foreign loves! —
Ay, there's the fruit he planted! never look
Astonished at me with your mother's eyes,
For it was they who set you where you are,
An undowered orphan.   Child, your father's choice
Of that said mother disinherited
His daughter, his and hers.   Men do not think
Of sons and daughters, when they fall in love,
So much more than of sisters; otherwise   610
He would have paused to ponder what he did,

And shrunk before that clause in the entail
Excluding offspring by a foreign wife
(The clause set up a hundred years ago
By a Leigh who wedded a French dancing-girl
And had his heart danced over in return) ;
But this man shrank at nothing, never thought
Of you, Aurora, any more than me —
Your mother must have been a pretty thing,
For all the coarse Italian blacks and browns,   620
To make a good man, which my brother was,
Unchary of the duties to his house ;
But so it fell indeed.   Our cousin Vane,
Vane Leigh, the father of this Romney, wrote
Directly on your birth, to Italy,
' I ask your baby daughter for my son,
In whom the entail now merges by the law.
Betroth her to us out of love, instead
Of colder reasons, and she shall not lose
By love or law from henceforth ' — so he wrote ; 630
A generous cousin was my cousin Vane.
Remember how he drew you to his knee
The year you came here, just before he died,
And hollowed out his hands to hold your cheeks,
And wished them redder, — you remember Vane.
And now his son, who represents our house,
And holds the fiefs and manors in his place,
To whom reverts my pittance when I die
(Except a few books and a pair of shawls),
The boy is generous like him, and prepared   640
To carry out his kindest word and thought
To you, Aurora.   Yes, a fine young man
Is Romney Leigh ; although the sun of youth
Has shone too straight upon his brain, I know,
And fevered him with dreams of doing good

To good-for-nothing people.   But a wife
Will put all right, and stroke his temples cool
With healthy touches." . . .

                        I broke in at that.
I could not lift my heavy heart to breathe
Till then, but then I raised it, and it fell   650
In broken words like these — " No need to wait :
The dream of doing good to . . . me, at least,
Is ended, without waiting for a wife
To cool the fever for him.   We've escaped
That danger, — thank Heaven for it."

                        " You," she cried,
" Have got a fever.   What, I talk and talk
An hour long to you, — I instruct you how
You cannot eat or drink or stand or sit
Or even die, like any decent wretch
In all this unroofed and unfurnished world,   660
Without your cousin, — and you still maintain
There's room 'twixt him and you for flirting fans
And running knots in eyebrows ?   You must have
A pattern lover sighing on his knee ?
You do not count enough, a noble heart
(Above book-patterns) which this very morn
Unclosed itself in two dear fathers' names
To embrace your orphaned life ?   Fie, fie ! But stay,
I write a word, and counteract this sin."

She would have turned to leave me, but I clung. 670
" O sweet my father's sister, hear my word
Before you write yours.   Cousin Vane did well,
And cousin Romney well, — and I well too,
In casting back with all my strength and will
The good they meant me.   O my God, my God !
God meant me good, too, when He hindered me

From saying 'yes' this morning.   If you write
A word, it shall be 'no.'   I say no, no !
I tie up 'no' upon His altar-horns,
Quite out of reach of perjury !   At least   680
My soul is not a pauper ; I can live
At least my soul's life, without alms from men ;
And if it must be in heaven instead of earth,
Let heaven look to it, — I am not afraid."

She seized my hands with both hers, strained them fast,
And drew her probing and unscrupulous eyes
Right through me, body and heart.   " Yet, foolish
          Sweet,
You love this man.   I've watched you when he came,
And when he went, and when we've talked of him :
I am not old for nothing ; I can tell   690
The weather-signs of love : you love this man."

Girls blush sometimes because they are alive,
Half wishing they were dead to save the shame.
The sudden blush devours them, neck and brow ;
They have drawn too near the fire of life, like gnats,
And flare up bodily, wings and all.   What then ?
Who's sorry for a gnat . . . or girl ?
                                                  I blushed.
I feel the brand upon my forehead now
Strike hot, sear deep, as guiltless men may feel
The felon's iron, say, and scorn the mark   700
Of what they are not.   Most illogical
Irrational nature of our womanhood,
That blushes one way, feels another way,
And prays, perhaps another !   After all,
We cannot be the equal of the male
Who rules his blood a little.

For although
I blushed indeed, as if I loved the man,
And her incisive smile, accrediting
That treason of false witness in my blush,
Did bow me downward like a swathe of grass   710
Below its level that struck me, — I attest
The conscious skies and all their daily suns,
I think I loved him not, — nor then, nor since,
Nor ever.   Do we love the schoolmaster,
Being busy in the woods ? much less, being poor,
The overseer of the parish ?   Do we keep
Our love to pay our debts with ?

                                        White and cold
I grew next moment.   As my blood recoiled
From that imputed ignominy, I made
My heart great with it.   Then, at last, I spoke,   720
Spoke veritable words but passionate,
Too passionate perhaps . . . ground up with sobs
To shapeless endings.   She let fall my hands
And took her smile off, in sedate disgust,
As peradventure she had touched a snake, —
A dead snake, mind ! — and, turning round, replied,
" We'll leave Italian manners, if you please.
I think you had an English father, child,
And ought to find it possible to speak
A quiet ' yes ' or ' no,' like English girls,   730
Without convulsions.   In another month
We'll take another answer — no, or yes."
With that, she left me in the garden-walk.

I had a father ! yes, but long ago —
How long it seemed that moment.   Oh, how far,
How far and safe, God, dost thou keep thy saints
When once gone from us !   We may call against

The lighted windows of thy fair June-heaven
Where all the souls are happy,— and not one,
Not even my father, look from work or play   740
To ask, " Who is it that cries after us,
Below there, in the dusk ? "   Yet formerly
He turned his face upon me quick enough,
If I said " Father."   Now I might cry loud ;
The little lark reached higher with his song
Than I with crying.   Oh, alone, alone,—
Not troubling any in heaven, nor any on earth,
I stood there in the garden, and looked up
The deaf blue sky that brings the roses out
On such June mornings.
                You who keep account 750
Of crisis and transition in this life,
Set down the first time Nature says plain " no "
To some " yes " in you, and walks over you
In gorgeous sweeps of scorn.   We all begin
By singing with the birds, and running fast
With June-days, hand in hand : but once, for all,
The birds must sing against us, and the sun
Strike down upon us like a friend's sword caught
By an enemy to slay us, while we read
The dear name on the blade which bites at us !— 760
That's bitter and convincing : after that,
We seldom doubt that something in the large
Smooth order of creation, though no more
Than haply a man's footstep, has gone wrong.
Some tears fell down my cheeks, and then I smiled,
As those smile who have no face in the world
To smile back to them.   I had lost a friend
In Romney Leigh ; the thing was sure — a friend,
Who had looked at me most gently now and then,
And spoken of my favourite books, " our books," 770

With such a voice ! Well, voice and look were now
More utterly shut out from me I felt,
Than even my father's. Romney now was turned
To a benefactor, to a generous man,
Who had tied himself to marry . . . me, instead
Of such a woman, with low timorous lids
He lifted with a sudden word one day,
And left, perhaps, for my sake. — Ah, self-tied
By a contract, male Iphigenia bound
At a fatal Aulis for the winds to change   780
(But loose him, they'll not change), he well might
      seem
A little cold and dominant in love !
He had a right to be dogmatical,
This poor, good Romney. Love, to him, was made
A simple law-clause. If I married him,
I should not dare to call my soul my own
Which so he had bought and paid for : every thought
And every heart-beat down there in the bill ;
Not one found honestly deductible
From any use that pleased him ! He might cut   790
My body into coins to give away
Among his other paupers ; change my sons,
While I stood dumb as Griseld, for black babes
Or piteous foundlings ; might unquestioned set
My right hand teaching in the Ragged Schools,
My left hand washing in the Public Baths,
What time my angel of the Ideal stretched
Both his to me in vain. I could not claim
The poor right of a mouse in a trap, to squeal,
And take so much as pity from myself.   800

Farewell, good Romney ! if I loved you even
I could but ill afford to let you be

So generous to me.   Farewell, friend, since friend
Betwixt us two, forsooth, must be a word
So heavily overladen.   And, since help
Must come to me from those who love me not,
Farewell, all helpers — I must help myself,
And am alone from henceforth. — Then I stooped
And lifted the soiled garland from the earth,
And set it on my head as bitterly   810
As when the Spanish monarch crowned the bones
Of his dead love.   So be it.   I preserve
That crown still, — in the drawer there ! twas the
      first.
The rest are like it ; — those Olympian crowns,
We run for, till we lose sight of the sun
In the dust of the racing chariots !
                                      After that,
Before the evening fell, I had a note,
Which ran, — " Aurora, sweet Chaldean, you read
My meaning backward like your eastern books,
While I am from the west, dear.   Read me now 820
A little plainer.   Did you hate me quite
But yesterday ?   I loved you for my part ;
I love you.   If I spoke untenderly
This morning, my beloved, pardon it ;
And comprehend me that I loved you so
I set you on the level of my soul,
And overwashed you with the bitter brine
Of some habitual thoughts.   Henceforth, my flower,
Be planted out of reach of any such,   829
And lean the side you please, with all your leaves !
Write woman's verses and dream woman's dreams ;
But let me feel your perfume in my home
To make my sabbath after working-days.
Bloom out your youth beside me, — be my wife."

I wrote in answer — "We Chaldeans discern
Still farther than we read.   I know your heart,
And shut it like the holy book it is,
Reserved for mild-eyed saints to pore upon
Betwixt their prayers at vespers.   Well, you're right,
I did not surely hate you yesterday ;   840
And yet I do not love you enough to-day
To wed you, cousin Romney.   Take this word,
And let it stop you as a generous man
From speaking farther.   You may tease, indeed,
And blow about my feelings, or my leaves,
And here's my aunt will help you with east winds
And break a stalk, perhaps, tormenting me ;
But certain flowers grow near as deep as trees,
And, cousin, you'll not move my root, not you, 849
With all your confluent storms.   Then let me grow
Within my wayside hedge, and pass your way !
This flower has never as much to say to you
As the antique tomb which said to travellers, ' Pause,
' Siste, viator.' "   Ending thus, I sighed.

The next week passed in silence, so the next,
And several after : Romney did not come
Nor my aunt chide me.   I lived on and on,
As if my heart were kept beneath a glass,
And everybody stood, all eyes and ears,
To see and hear it tick.   I could not sit,   860
Nor walk, nor take a book, nor lay it down,
Nor sew on steadily, nor drop a stitch,
And a sigh with it, but I felt her looks
Still cleaving to me, like the sucking asp
To Cleopatra's breast, persistently
Through the intermittent pantings.   Being observed,
When observation is not sympathy,

Is just being tortured.   If she said a word,
A "thank you," or an "if it please you, dear,"
She meant a commination, or, at best,   870
An exorcism against the devildom
Which plainly held me.   So with all the house.
Susannah could not stand and twist my hair
Without such glancing at the looking-glass
To see my face there, that she missed the plait.
And John, — I never sent my plate for soup,
Or did not send it, but the foolish John
Resolved the problem, 'twixt his napkined thumbs,
Of what was signified by taking soup   879
Or choosing mackerel.   Neighbours who dropped in
On morning visits, feeling a joint wrong,
Smiled admonition, sat uneasily,
And talked, with measured, emphasised reserve,
Of parish news, like doctors to the sick,
When not called in, — as if, with leave to speak,
They might say something.   Nay, the very dog
Would watch me from his sun-patch on the floor,
In alternation with the large black fly
Not yet in reach of snapping.   So I lived.

A Roman died so ; smeared with honey, teased   890
By insects, stared to torture by the moon :
And many patient souls 'neath English roofs
Have died like Romans.   I, in looking back,
Wish only, now, I had borne the plague of all
With meeker spirits than were rife at Rome.

For, on the sixth week, the dead sea broke up,
Dashed suddenly through beneath the heel of Him
Who stands upon the sea and earth and swears
Time shall be nevermore.   The clock struck nine

That morning too, — no lark was out of tune,   900
The hidden farms among the hills breathed straight
Their smoke toward heaven, the lime-tree scarcely
    stirred
Beneath the blue weight of the cloudless sky,
Though still the July air came floating through
The woodbine at my window, in and out,
With touches of the out-door country news
For a bending forehead.   There I sat, and wished
That morning-truce of God would last till eve,
Or longer.   "Sleep," I thought, "late sleepers, —
    sleep,
And spare me yet the burden of your eyes."   910

Then, suddenly, a single ghastly shriek
Tore upward from the bottom of the house.
Like one who wakens in a grave and shrieks,
The still house seemed to shriek itself alive,
And shudder through its passages and stairs
With slam of doors and clash of bells. — I sprang,
I stood up in the middle of the room,
And there confronted at my chamber-door
A white face, — shivering, ineffectual lips.   919

" Come, come," they tried to utter, and I went :
As if a ghost had drawn me at the point
Of a fiery finger through the uneven dark,
I went with reeling footsteps down the stair,
Nor asked a question.
                        There she sat, my aunt, —
Bolt upright in the chair beside her bed,
Whose pillow had no dint ! she had used no bed
For that night's sleeping, yet slept well.   My God,
The dumb derision of that grey, peaked face

Concluded something grave against the sun,
Which filled the chamber with its July burst   930
When Susan drew the curtains ignorant
Of who sat open-eyed behind her.   There
She sat . . . it sat . . . we said "she" yester-
      day . . .
And held a letter with unbroken seal
As Susan gave it to her hand last night :
All night she had held it.   If its news referred
To duchies or to dunghills, not an inch
She'd budge, 'twas obvious, for such worthless odds :
Nor, though the stars were suns and overburned
Their spheric limitations, swallowing up   940
Like wax the azure spaces, could they force
Those open eyes to wink once.   What last sight
Had left them blank and flat so, — drawing out
The faculty of vision from the roots,
As nothing more, worth seeing, remained behind ?

Were those the eyes that watched me, worried me ?
That dogged me up and down the hours and days,
A beaten, breathless, miserable soul ?
And did I pray, a half-hour back, but so,   949
To escape the burden of those eyes . . . those eyes ?
"Sleep late" I said ? —
                    Why, now, indeed, they sleep.
God answers sharp and sudden on some prayers,
And thrusts the thing we have prayed for in our face,
A gauntlet with a gift in't.   Every wish
Is like a prayer, with God.
                    I had my wish,
To read and meditate the thing I would,
To fashion all my life upon my thought,
And marry or not marry.   Henceforth none

Could disapprove me, vex me, hamper me.
Full ground-room, in this desert newly made,   960
For Babylon or Baalbec, — when the breath,
Now choked with sand, returns for building towns.

The heir came over on the funeral day,
And we two cousins met before the dead,
With two pale faces.   Was it death or life
That moved us ?   When the will was read and done,
The official guests and witnesses withdrawn,
We rose up in a silence almost hard,
And looked at one another.   Then I said,
" Farewell, my cousin."
                              But he touched, just touched 970
My hatstrings, tied for going (at the door
The carriage stood to take me), and said low,
His voice a little unsteady through his smile,
" Siste, viator."
                    " Is there time," I asked,
" In these last days of railroads, to stop short
Like Cæsar's chariot (weighing half a ton)
On the Appian road, for morals ? "
                                    " There is time,"
He answered grave, " for necessary words,
Inclusive, trust me, of no epitaph
On man or act, my cousin.   We have read   980
A will, which gives you all the personal goods
And funded moneys of your aunt."
                                    " I thank
Her memory for it.   With three hundred pounds
We buy, in England even, clear standing-room
To stand and work in.   Only two hours since,
I fancied I was poor."
                        " And, cousin, still

You're richer than you fancy.   The will says,
Three hundred pounds, and any other sum
Of which the said testatrix dies possessed.
I say she died possessed of other sums."   990

" Dear Romney, need we chronicle the pence ?
I'm richer than I thought — that's evident.
Enough so."
                   " Listen rather.   You've to do
With business and a cousin," he resumed,
" And both, I fear, need patience.   Here's the fact.
The other sum (there *is* another sum,
Unspecified in any will which dates
After possession, yet bequeathed as much
And clearly as those said three hundred pounds)
Is thirty thousand.   You will have it paid   1000
When ? . . . where ?   My duty troubles you with
      words."

He struck the iron when the bar was hot ;
No wonder if my eyes sent out some sparks.
" Pause there ! I thank you.   You are delicate
In glosing gifts ; — but I, who share your blood,
Am rather made for giving, like yourself,
Than taking, like your pensioners.   Farewell."

He stopped me with a gesture of calm pride.
" A Leigh," he said, " gives largesse and gives love,
But gloses never : if a Leigh could glose,   1010
He would not do it, moreover, to a Leigh,
With blood trained up along nine centuries
To hound and hate a lie from eyes like yours.
And now we'll make the rest as clear : your aunt
Possessed these moneys."
                          " You will make it clear,

My cousin, as the honour of us both,
Or one of us speaks vainly ! that's not I.
My aunt possessed this sum, — inherited
From whom, and when ? bring documents, prove
    dates.''

" Why now indeed you throw your bonnet off 1020
As if you had time left for a logarithm !
The faith's the want.   Dear cousin, give me faith,
And you shall walk this road with silken shoes,
As clean as any lady of our house
Supposed the proudest.   Oh, I comprehend
The whole position from your point of sight.
I oust you from your father's halls and lands
And make you poor by getting rich — that's law ;
Considering which, in common circumstance,
You would not scruple to accept from me 1030
Some compensation, some sufficiency
Of income — that were justice ; but, alas,
I love you, — that's mere nature ; you reject
My love, — that's nature also ; and at once,
You cannot, from a suitor disallowed,
A hand thrown back as mine is, into yours
Receive a doit, a farthing, — not for the world !
That's woman's etiquette, and obviously
Exceeds the claim of nature, law, and right,
Unanswerable to all.   I grant, you see, 1040
The case as you conceive it, — leave you room
To sweep your ample skirts of womanhood,
While, standing humbly squeezed against the wall,
I own myself excluded from being just,
Restrained from paying indubitable debts,
Because denied from giving you my soul.
That's my misfortune ! — I submit to it

As if, in some more reasonable age,
'Twould not be less inevitable.   Enough.
You'll trust me, cousin, as a gentleman,   1050
To keep your honour, as you count it, pure,
Your scruples (just as if I thought them wise)
Safe and inviolate from gifts of mine.''
I answered mild but earnest.   "I believe
In no one's honour which another keeps,
Nor man's nor woman's.   As I keep, myself,
My truth and my religion, I depute
No father, though I had one this side death,   1058
Nor brother, though I had twenty, much less you,
Though twice my cousin, and once Romney Leigh,
To keep my honour pure.   Your face, to-day,
A man who wants instruction, mark me, not
A woman who wants protection.   As to a man,
Show manhood, speak out plainly, be precise
With facts and dates.   My aunt inherited
This sum, you say —— ''

                            "I said she died possessed
Of this, dear cousin.''

                            "Not by heritage.
Thank you : we're getting to the facts at last.
Perhaps she played at commerce with a ship
Which came in heavy with Australian gold ?   1070
Or touched a lottery with her finger-end,
Which tumbled on a sudden into her lap
Some old Rhine tower or principality ?
Perhaps she had to do with a marine
Sub-transatlantic railroad, which pre-pays
As well as pre-supposes ? or perhaps
Some stale ancestral debt was after-paid
By a hundred years, and took her by surprise ? ——
You shake your head, my cousin ; I guess ill.''

" You need not guess, Aurora, nor deride ;   1080
The truth is not afraid of hurting you.
You'll find no cause, in all your scruples, why
Your aunt should cavil at a deed of gift
'Twixt her and me."

           " I thought so — ah ! a gift."

" You naturally thought so," he resumed.
" A very natural gift."

           " A gift, a gift !
Her individual life being stranded high
Above all want, approaching opulence,
Too haughty was she to accept a gift
Without some ultimate aim : ah, ah, I see, —   1090
A gift intended plainly for her heirs,
And so accepted . . . if accepted . . . ah,
Indeed that might be ; I am snared perhaps
Just so.   But, cousin, shall I pardon you,
If thus you have caught me with a cruel springe ? "

He answered gently, " Need you tremble and pant
Like a netted lioness ? is't my fault, mine,
That you're a grand wild creature of the woods
And hate the stall built for you ?   Any way,
Though triply netted, need you glare at me ?   1100
I do not hold the cords of such a net ;
You're free from me, Aurora ! "

           " Now may God
Deliver me from this strait !   This gift of yours
Was tendered . . . when ? accepted . . . when ? "
    I asked.
" A month . . . a fortnight since ?   Six weeks ago
It was not tendered ; by a word she dropped
I know it was not tendered nor received.

When was it ? bring your dates."

                " What matters when ?
A half-hour ere she died, or a half-year,
Secured the gift, maintains the heritage   1110
Inviolable with law.   As easy pluck
The golden stars from heaven's embroidered stole
To pin them on the grey side of this earth,
As make you poor again, thank God."

                    " Not poor
Nor clean again from henceforth, you thank God ?
Well, sir — I ask you — I insist at need, —
Vouchsafe the special date, the special date."

" The day before her death-day," he replied,
" The gift was in her hands.   We'll find that deed,
And certify that date to you."

                   As one   1120
Who has climbed a mountain-height and carried up
His own heart climbing, panting in his throat
With the toil of the ascent, takes breath at last,
Looks back in triumph — so I stood and looked.
" Dear cousin Romney, we have reached the top
Of this steep question, and may rest, I think.
But first, — I pray you pardon, that the shock
And surge of natural feeling and event
Has made me oblivious of acquainting you   1129
That this, this letter (unread, mark, still sealed),
Was found enfolded in the poor dead hand :
That spirit of hers had gone beyond the address,
Which could not find her though you wrote it clear, —
I know your writing, Romney, — recognise
The open-hearted *A*, the liberal sweep
Of the *G*.   Now listen, — let us understand :
You will not find that famous deed of gift,

Unless you find it in the letter here,
Which, not being mine, I give you back. — Refuse
To take the letter? well then — you and I,   1140
As writer and as heiress, open it
Together, by your leave. —— Exactly so :
The words in which the noble offering's made
Are nobler still, my cousin ; and, I own,
The proudest and most delicate heart alive,
Distracted from the measure of the gift
By such a grace in giving, might accept
Your largesse without thinking any more
Of the burthen of it, than King Solomon
Considered, when he wore his holy ring   1150
Charactered over with the ineffable spell,
How many carats of fine gold made up
Its money-value : so, Leigh gives to Leigh !
Or rather, might have given, observe, — for that's
The point we come to.   Here's a proof of gift,
But here's no proof, sir, of acceptancy,
But, rather, disproof. Death's black dust, being blown,
Infiltrated through every secret fold
Of this sealed letter by a puff of fate,
Dried up for ever the fresh-written ink,   1160
Annulled the gift, disutilized the grace,
And left these fragments."
                              As I spoke, I tore
The paper up and down, and down and up
And crosswise, till it fluttered from my hands,
As forest-leaves, stripped suddenly and rapt
By a whirlwind on Valdarno, drop again,
Drop slow, and strew the melancholy ground
Before the amazèd hills . . . why, so, indeed,
I'm writing like a poet, somewhat large
In the type of the image, and exaggerate   1170

A small thing with a great thing, topping it : —
But then I'm thinking how his eyes looked, his,
With what despondent and surprised reproach !
I think the tears were in them as he looked ;
I think the manly mouth just trembled.   Then
He broke the silence.

                        " I may ask, perhaps,
Although no stranger . . . only Romney Leigh,
Which means still less . . . than Vincent Carring-
    ton,
Your plans in going hence, and where you go.
This cannot be a secret."

                         " All my life   1180
Is open to you, cousin.   I go hence
To London, to the gathering-place of souls,
To live mine straight out, vocally, in books ;
Harmoniously for others, if indeed
A woman's soul, like man's, be wide enough
To carry the whole octave (that's to prove),
Or, if I fail, still purely for myself.
Pray God be with me, Romney."

                         " Ah, poor child,
Who fight against the mother's 'tiring hand,
And choose the headsman's !   May God change His
    world   1190
For your sake, sweet, and make it mild as heaven,
And juster than I have found you."

                         But I paused.
" And you, my cousin ? " —
                         " I," he said, — " you ask ?
You care to ask ?   Well, girls have curious minds
And fain would know the end of everything,
Of cousins therefore with the rest.   For me,
Aurora, I've my work ; you know my work ;

And, having missed this year some personal hope,
I must beware the rather that I miss
No reasonable duty.   While you sing   1200
Your happy pastorals of the meads and trees,
Bethink you that I go to impress and prove
On stifled brains and deafened ears, stunned deaf,
Crushed dull with grief, that nature sings itself,
And needs no mediate poet, lute or voice,
To make it vocal.   While you ask of men
Your audience, I may get their leave perhaps
For hungry orphans to say audibly
' We're hungry, see,' — for beaten and bullied
     wives
To hold their unweaned babies up in sight,   1210
Whom orphanage would better, and for all
To speak and claim their portion . . . by no means
Of the soil, . . . but of the sweat in tilling it ;
Since this is nowadays turned privilege,
To have only God's curse on us, and not man's.
Such work I have for doing, elbow-deep
In social problems, — as you tie your rhymes,
To draw my uses to cohere with needs
And bring the uneven world back to its round,
Or, failing so much, fill up, bridge at least   1220
To smoother issues some abysmal cracks
And feuds of earth, intestine heats have made
To keep men separate, — using sorry shifts
Of hospitals, almshouses, infant schools,
And other practical stuff of partial good
You lovers of the beautiful and whole
Despise by system."
                              " I despise ?   The scorn
Is yours, my cousin.   Poets become such
Through scorning nothing.   You decry them for

The good of beauty sung and taught by them,   1230
While they respect your practical partial good
As being a part of beauty's self.   Adieu !
When God helps all the workers for His world,
The singers shall have help of Him, not last."

He smiled as men smile when they will not speak
Because of something bitter in the thought ;
And still I feel his melancholy eyes
Look judgment on me.   It is seven years since:
I know not if 'twas pity or 'twas scorn
Has made them so far-reaching : judge it ye   1240
Who have had to do with pity more than love
And scorn than hatred.   I am used, since then,
To other ways, from equal men.   But so,
Even so, we let go hands, my cousin and I,
And in between us rushed the torrent-world
To blanch our faces like divided rocks,
And bar for ever mutual sight and touch
Except through swirl of spray and all that roar.

THIRD BOOK.

"To—day thou girdest up thy loins thyself
And goest where thou wouldest : presently
Others shall gird thee," said the Lord, " to go
Where thou wouldst not."   He spoke to Peter
     thus,
To signify the death which he should die
When crucified head downward.

                              If He spoke
To Peter then, He speaks to us the same ;
The word suits many different martyrdoms,

And signifies a multiform of death,
Although we scarcely die apostles, we,　　　　10
And have mislaid the keys of heaven and earth.

For 'tis not in mere death that men die most,
And, after our first girding of the loins
In youth's fine linen and fair broidery
To run up hill and meet the rising sun,
We are apt to sit tired, patient as a fool,
While others gird us with the violent bands
Of social figments, feints, and formalisms,
Reversing our straight nature, lifting up
Our base needs, keeping down our lofty thoughts,　20
Head downward on the cross-sticks of the world.
Yet He can pluck us from that shameful cross.
God, set our feet low and our forehead high,
And show us how a man was made to walk !

Leave the lamp, Susan, and go up to bed.
The room does very well ; I have to write
Beyond the stroke of midnight.　Get away ;
Your steps, for ever buzzing in the room,
Tease me like gnats.　Ah, letters ! throw them down
At once, as I must have them, to be sure,　　　30
Whether I bid you never bring me such
At such an hour, or bid you.　No excuse ;
You choose to bring them, as I choose perhaps
To throw them in the fire.　Now get to bed,
And dream, if possible, I am not cross.

Why what a pettish, petty thing I grow, —
A mere mere woman, a mere flaccid nerve,
A kerchief left out all night in the rain,
Turned soft so, — overtasked and overstrained

And overlived in this close London life !   40
And yet I should be stronger.
                              Never burn
Your letters, poor Aurora ! for they stare
With red seals from the table, saying each,
" Here's something that you know not." Out, alas,
'Tis scarcely that the world's more good and wise
Or even straighter and more consequent
Since yesterday at this time — yet, again,
If but one angel spoke from Ararat
I should be very sorry not to hear :
So open all the letters ! let me read.   50
Blanche Ord, the writer in the " Lady's Fan,"
Requests my judgment on . . . that, afterwards.
Kate Ward desires the model of my cloak,
And signs " Elisha to you." Pringle Sharpe
Presents his work on " Social Conduct," craves
A little money for his pressing debts . . .
From me, who scarce have money for my needs ;
Art's fiery chariot which we journey in
Being apt to singe our singing-robes to holes,
Although you ask me for my cloak, Kate Ward !   60
Here's Rudgely knows it, — editor and scribe ;
He's " forced to marry where his heart is not,
Because the purse lacks where he lost his heart."
Ah, —— lost it because no one picked it up ;
That's really loss, — (and passable impudence).
My critic Hammond flatters prettily,
And wants another volume like the last.
My critic Belfair wants another book
Entirely different, which will sell (and live ?),
A striking book, yet not a startling book,   70
The public blames originalities
(You must not pump spring-water unawares

Upon a gracious public full of nerves) :
Good things, not subtle, new yet orthodox,
As easy reading as the dog-eared page
That's fingered by said public fifty years,
Since first taught spelling by its grandmother,
And yet a revelation in some sort :
That's hard, my critic Belfair.   So — what next ?
My critic Stokes objects to abstract thoughts ;   80
" Call a man John, a woman Joan," says he,
" And do not prate so of *humanities:* "
Whereat I call my critic simply, Stokes.
My critic Jobson recommends more mirth
Because a cheerful genius suits the times,
And all true poets laugh unquenchably
Like Shakespeare and the gods.   That's very hard.
The gods may laugh, and Shakespeare ; Dante smiled
With such a needy heart on two pale lips,
We cry " Weep rather, Dante."   Poems are   90
Men, if true poems : and who dares exclaim
At any man's door, " Here, 'tis understood
The thunder fell last week and killed a wife
And scared a sickly husband — what of that ?
Get up, be merry, shout and clap your hands,
Because a cheerful genius suits the times — " ?
None says so to the man, and why indeed
Should any to the poem ?   A ninth seal ;
The apocalypse is drawing to a close.
Ha, — this from Vincent Carrington, — " Dear
        friend,   100
I want good counsel.   Will you lend me wings
To raise me to the subject, in a sketch
I'll bring to-morrow — may I ? at eleven ?
A poet's only born to turn to use :
So save you ! for the world . . . and Carrington."

" (Writ after.)   Have you heard of Romney Leigh,
Beyond what's said of him in newspapers,
His phalansteries there, his speeches here,
His pamphlets, pleas, and statements, everywhere ?
He dropped *me* long ago, but no one drops   110
A golden apple — though indeed one day
You hinted that, but jested.   Well, at least
You know Lord Howe who sees him . . . whom he
      sees
And *you* see and I hate to see, — for Howe
Stands high upon the brink of theories,
Observes the swimmers and cries ' Very fine,'
But keeps dry linen equally, — unlike
That gallant breaster, Romney.   Strange it is,
Such sudden madness seizing a young man
To make earth over again, — while I'm content   120
To make the pictures.   Let me bring the sketch.
A tiptoe Danae, overbold and hot,
Both arms a-flame to meet her wishing Jove
Halfway, and burn him faster down ; the face
And breasts upturned and straining, the loose locks
All glowing with the anticipated gold.
Or here's another on the self-same theme.
She lies here — flat upon her prison-floor,
The long hair swathed about her to the heel
Like wet seaweed.   You dimly see her through   130
The glittering haze of that prodigious rain,
Half blotted out of nature by a love
As heavy as fate.   I'll bring you either sketch.
I think, myself, the second indicates
More passion."
                        Surely.   Self is put away,
And calm with abdication.   She is Jove,
And no more Danae — greater thus.   Perhaps

The painter symbolises unaware
Two states of the recipient artist-soul,
One, forward, personal, wanting reverence,   140
Because aspiring only.   We'll be calm,
And know that, when indeed our Joves come down,
We all turn stiller than we have ever been.

Kind Vincent Carrington.   I'll let him come.
He talks of Florence, — and may say a word
Of something as it chanced seven years ago,
A hedgehog in the path, or a lame bird,
In those green country walks, in that good time
When certainly I was so miserable . . .
I seemed to have missed a blessing ever since.   150

The music soars within the little lark,
And the lark soars.   It is not thus with men.
We do not make our places with our strains, —
Content, while they rise, to remain behind
Alone on earth instead of so in heaven.
No matter ; I bear on my broken tale.

When Romney Leigh and I had parted thus,
I took a chamber up three flights of stairs
Not far from being as steep as some larks climb,
And there, in a certain house in Kensington,   160
Three years I lived and worked.   Get leave to work
In this world — 'tis the best you get at all ;
For God, in cursing, gives us better gifts
Than men in benediction.   God says, " Sweat
For foreheads," men say " crowns," and so we are
        crowned,
Ay, gashed by some tormenting circle of steel

Which snaps with a secret spring.   Get work, get
    work ;
Be sure 'tis better than what you work to get.

Serene and unafraid of solitude,   169
I worked the short days out, — and watched the sun
On lurid morns or monstrous afternoons
(Like some Druidic idol's fiery brass
With fixed unflickering outline of dead heat,
From which the blood of wretches pent inside
Seems oozing forth to incarnadine the air)
Push out through fog with his dilated disk,
And startle the slant roofs and chimney-pots
With splashes of fierce colour.   Or I saw
Fog only, the great tawny weltering fog,
Involve the passive city, strangle it   180
Alive, and draw it off into the void,
Spires, bridges, streets, and squares, as if a sponge
Had wiped out London, — or as noon and night
Had clapped together and utterly struck out
The intermediate time, undoing themselves
In the act.   Your city poets see such things
Not despicable.   Mountains of the south,
When drunk and mad with elemental wines
They rend the seamless mist and stand up bare,
Make fewer singers, haply.   No one sings,   190
Descending Sinai : on Parnassus mount
You take a mule to climb and not a muse
Except in fable and figure : forests chant
Their anthems to themselves, and leave you dumb.
But sit in London at the day's decline,
And view the city perish in the mist
Like Pharaoh's armaments in the deep Red Sea,
The chariots, horsemen, footmen, all the host,

Sucked down and choked to silence — then, surprised
By a sudden sense of vision and of tune,   200
You feel as conquerors though you did not fight,
And you and Israel's other singing girls,
Ay, Miriam with them, sing the song you choose.
I worked with patience, which means almost power :
I did some excellent things indifferently,
Some bad things excellently.   Both were praised,
The latter loudest.   And by such a time
That I myself had set them down as sins
Scarce worth the price of sackcloth, week by week
Arrived some letter through the sedulous post,   210
Like these I've read, and yet dissimilar,
With pretty maiden seals, — initials twined
Of lilies, or a heart marked *Emily*
(Convicting Emily of being all heart) ;
Or rarer tokens from young bachelors,
Who wrote from college with the same goosequill,
Suppose, they had just been plucked of, and a snatch
From Horace, " Collegisse juvat," set
Upon the first page.   Many a letter, signed
Or unsigned, showing the writers at eighteen   220
Had lived too long, although a muse should help
Their dawn by holding candles, — compliments
To smile or sigh at.   Such could pass with me
No more than coins from Moscow circulate
At Paris : would ten roubles buy a tag
Of ribbon on the boulevard, worth a sou ?
I smiled that all this youth should love me, — sighed
That such a love could scarcely raise them up
To love what was more worthy than myself;
Then sighed again, again, less generously,   230
To think the very love they lavish so
Proved me inferior.   The strong loved me not,

And he . . . my cousin Romney . . . did not
    write.
I felt the silent finger of his scorn
Prick every bubble of my frivolous fame
As my breath blew it, and resolve it back
To the air it came from.   Oh, I justified
The measure he had taken of my height :
The thing was plain — he was not wrong a line ;
I played at art, made thrusts with a toy-sword,   240
Amused the lads and maidens.

                       Came a sigh
Deep, hoarse with resolution, — I would work
To better ends, or play in earnest.   " Heavens,
I think I should be almost popular
If this went on ! " — I ripped my verses up,
And found no blood upon the rapier's point ;
The heart in them was just an embryo's heart
Which never yet had beat, that it should die ;
Just gasps of make-believe galvanic life ;
Mere tones, inorganised to any tune.   250

And yet I felt it in me where it burnt,
Like those hot fire-seeds of creation held
In Jove's clenched palm before the worlds were sown, —
But I — I was not Juno even ! my hand
Was shut in weak convulsion, woman's ill,
And when I yearned to loose a finger — lo,
The nerve revolted.   'Tis the same even now :
This hand may never, haply, open large,
Before the spark is quenched, or the palm charred,
To prove the power not else by the pain.   260

It burnt, it burns — my whole life burnt with it,
And light, not sunlight and not torchlight, flashed

My steps out through the slow and difficult road.
I had grown distrustful of too forward Springs,
The season's books in drear significance
Of morals, dropping round me.   Lively books ?
The ash has livelier verdure than the yew ;
And yet the yew's green longer, and alone
Found worthy of the holy Christmas time :
We'll plant more yews if possible, albeit   270
We plant the graveyards with them.

        Day and night
I worked my rhythmic thought, and furrowed up
Both watch and slumber with long lines of life
Which did not suit their season.   The rose fell
From either cheek, my eyes globed luminous
Through orbits of blue shadow, and my pulse
Would shudder along the purple-veinèd wrist
Like a shot bird.   Youth's stern, set face to face
With youth's ideal : and when people came   279
And said " You work too much, you are looking ill,"
I smiled for pity of them who pitied me,
Aud thought I should be better soon perhaps
For those ill looks.   Observe — " I," means in youth
Just *I*, the conscious and eternal soul
With all its ends, and not the outside life,
The parcel-man, the doublet of the flesh,
The so much liver, lung, integument,
Which make the sum of " I " hereafter when
World-talkers talk of doing well or ill.
I prosper if I gain a step, although   290
A nail then pierced my foot : although my brain
Embracing any truth froze paralysed,
I prosper : I but change my instrument ;
I break the spade off, digging deep for gold,
And catch the mattock up.

                                I worked on, on.
Through all the bristling fence of nights and days
Which hedges time in from the eternities,
I struggled, — never stopped to note the stakes
Which hurt me in my course.   The midnight oil
Would stink sometimes; there came some vulgar
        needs :   300
I had to live that therefore I might work,
And, being but poor, I was constrained, for life,
To work with one hand for the booksellers
While working with the other for myself
And art : you swim with feet as well as hands,
Or make small way.   I apprehended this, —
In England no one lives by verse that lives ;
And, apprehending, I resolved by prose
To make a space to sphere my living verse.
I wrote for cyclopædias, magazines,   310
And weekly papers, holding up my name
To keep it from the mud.   I learnt the use
Of the editorial " we " in a review
As courtly ladies the fine trick of trains,
And swept it grandly through the open doors
As if one could not pass through doors at all
Save so encumbered.   I wrote tales beside,
Carved many an article on cherry-stones
To suit light readers, — something in the lines
Revealing, it was said, the mallet-hand,   320
But that, I'll never vouch for : what you do
For bread will taste of common grain, not grapes,
Although you have a vineyard in Champagne ;
Much less in Nephelococcygia
As mine was, peradventure.
                                Having bread
For just so many days, just breathing-room

For body and verse, I stood up straight and worked
My veritable work.   And as the soul
Which grows within a child makes the child grow, —
Or as the fiery sap, the touch from God,   330
Careering through a tree, dilates the bark
And roughs with scale and knob, before it strikes
The summer foliage out in a green flame —
So life, in deepening with me, deepened all
The course I took, the work I did.   Indeed
The academic law convinced of sin ;
The critics cried out on the falling off,
Regretting the first manner.   But I felt
My heart's life throbbing in my verse to show
It lived, it also — certes incomplete,   340
Disordered with all Adam in the blood,
But even its very tumours, warts and wens
Still organised by and implying life.

A lady called upon me on such a day.
She had the low voice of your English dames,
Unused, it seems, to need rise half a note
To catch attention, — and their quiet mood,
As if they lived too high above the earth
For that to put them out in anything :
So gentle, because verily so proud ;   350
So wary and afraid of hurting you,
By no means that you are not really vile,
But that they would not touch you with their foot
To push you to your place ; so self-possessed
Yet gracious and conciliating, it takes
An effort in their presence to speak truth :
You know the sort of woman, — brilliant stuff,
And out of nature.   "Lady Waldemar."
She said her name quite simply, as if it meant   359

Not much indeed, but something, — took my hands,
And smiled as if her smile could help my case,
And dropped her eyes on me and let them melt.
" Is this," she said, " the Muse " ?

　　　　　　　　　　　　" No sybil even,"
I answered, " since she fails to guess the cause
Which taxed you with this visit, madam."

　　　　　　　　　　　　　　　　" Good,"
She said ; " I value what's sincere at once.
Perhaps if I had found a literal Muse,
The visit might have taxed me.　As it is,
You wear your blue so chiefly in your eyes,
My fair Aurora, in a frank good way,　　　　　　370
It comforts me entirely for your fame,
As well as for the trouble of ascent
To this Olympus."

　　　　　　　　　There, a silver laugh
Ran rippling through her quickened little breaths
The steep stair somewhat justified.

　　　　　　　　　　　　　" But still
Your ladyship has left me curious why
You dared the risk of finding the said Muse ? "

" Ah, — keep me, notwithstanding, to the point,
Like any pedant ?　Is the blue in eyes
As awful as in stockings after all,　　　　　　380
I wonder, that you'd have my business out
Before I breathe — exact the epic plunge
In spite of gasps ?　Well, naturally you think
I've come here, as the lion-hunters go
To deserts, to secure you with a trap
For exhibition in my drawing-rooms
On zoologic soirées ?　Not in the least.
Roar softly at me ; I am frivolous,

I dare say : I have played at wild-beast shows
Like other women of my class,— but now   390
I meet my lion simply as Androcles
Met his . . . when at his mercy.''

                       So, she bent
Her head, as queens may mock, — then lifting up
Her eyelids with a real grave queenly look,
Which ruled and would not spare, not even herself, —
'' I think you have a cousin : — Romney Leigh.''

'' You bring a word from *him ?* '' — my eyes leapt up
To the very height of hers, — '' a word from *him ?* ''

'' I bring a word about him, actually.   399
But first '' (she pressed me with her urgent eyes),
'' You do not love him, — you ?''
                      '' You're frank at least
In putting questions, madam,'' I replied ;
'' I love my cousin cousinly — no more.''

  '' I guessed as much.   I'm ready to be frank
In answering also, if you'll question me,
Or even for something less.   You stand outside,
You artist women, of the common sex ;
You share not with us, and exceed us so
Perhaps by what you're mulcted in, your hearts   409
Being starved to make your heads : so run the old
Traditions of you.   I can therefore speak
Without the natural shame which creatures feel
When speaking on their level, to their like.
There's many a papist she, would rather die
Than own to her maid she put a ribbon on
To catch the indifferent eye of such a man,
Who yet would count adulteries on her beads

At holy Mary's shrine and never blush ;
Because the saints are so far off, we lose
All modesty before them.   Thus, to-day.   420
'Tis *I*, love Romney Leigh."

                     " Forbear," I cried.
" If here's no Muse, still less is any saint ;
Nor even a friend, that Lady Waldemar
Should make confessions " . . .

                  " That's unkindly said :
If no friend, what forbids to make a friend
To join to our confession ere we have done ?
I love your cousin.   If it seems unwise
To say so, it's still foolisher (we're frank)
To feel so.   My first husband left me young,   429
And pretty enough, so please you, and rich enough,
To keep my booth in Mayfair with the rest
To happy issues.   There are marquises
Would serve seven years to call me wife, I know,
And, after seven, I might consider it,
For there's some comfort in a marquisate
When all's said, — yes, but after the seven years ;
I, now, love Romney.   You put up your lip,
So like a Leigh ! so like him ! — Pardon me,
I'm well aware I do not derogate
In loving Romney Leigh.   The name is good,   440
The means are excellent, but the man, the man —
Heaven help us both, — I am near as mad as he,
In loving such an one."

                   She slowly swung
Her heavy ringlets till they touched her smile,
As reasonably sorry for herself,
And thus continued.

                 " Of a truth, Miss Leigh,
I have not, without struggle, come to this.

I took a master in the German tongue,
I gamed a little, went to Paris twice ;
But, after all, this love ! . . . you eat of love,   450
And do as vile a thing as if you ate
Of garlic — which, whatever else you eat,
Tastes uniformly acrid, till your peach
Reminds you of your onion.   Am I coarse ?
Well, love's coarse, nature's coarse — ah, there's the
    rub.
We fair fine ladies, who park out our lives,
From common sheep-paths, cannot help the crows
From flying over, — we're as natural still
As Blowsalinda.   Drape us perfectly
In Lyons velvet, — we are not, for that,   460
Lay-figures, look you : we have hearts within,
Warm, live, improvident, indecent hearts,
As ready for outrageous ends and acts
As any distressed sempstress of them all
That Romney groans and toils for.   We catch love,
And other fevers, in the vulgar way :
Love will not be outwitted by our wit,
Nor outrun by our equipages : — mine
Persisted, spite of efforts.   All my cards   469
Turned up but Romney Leigh ; my German stopped
At germane Wertherism ; my Paris rounds
Returned me from the Champs Elysées just
A ghost, and sighing like Dido's.   I came home
Uncured, — convicted rather to myself
Of being in love . . . in love !   That's coarse, you'll
    say,
I'm talking garlic."
              Coldly I replied :
" Apologise for atheism, not love !
For me, I do believe in love, and God.

I know my cousin : Lady Waldemar
I know not : yet I say as much as this, —   480
Whoever loves him, let her not excuse
But cleanse herself, that, loving such a man,
She may not do it with such unworthy love
He cannot stoop and take it.''

                      '' That is said
Austerely, like a youthful prophetess,
Who knits her brows across her pretty eyes
To keep them back from following the grey flight
Of doves between the temple-columns.   Dear,
Be kinder with me ; let us two be friends.
I'm a mere woman, — the more weak perhaps   490
Through being so proud ; you're better ; as for him,
He's best.   Indeed he builds his goodness up
So high, it topples down to the other side
And makes a sort of badness ; there's the worst
I have to say against your cousin's best !
And so be mild, Aurora, with my worst
For his sake, if not mine.''

                     '' I own myself
Incredulous of confidence like this
Availing him or you.''

                 '' And I, myself,
Of being worthy of him with any love :   500
In your sense I am not so — let it pass.
And yet I save him if I marry him ;
Let that pass too.''

               '' Pass, pass ! we play police
Upon my cousin's life, to indicate
What may or may not pass ? '' I cried.   '' He knows
What's worthy of him ; the choice remains with *him* ;
And what he chooses, act or wife, I think
I shall not call unworthy, I, for one.''

" 'Tis somewhat rashly said," she answered slow ;
" Now let's talk reason, though we talk of love.   510
Your cousin Romney Leigh's a monster ; there,
The word's out fairly, let me prove the fact.
We'll take, say, that most perfect of antiques
They call the Genius of the Vatican
(Which seems too beauteous to endure itself
In this mixed world), and fasten it for once
Upon the torso of the Dancing Faun
(Who might limp surely, if he did not dance),
Instead of Buonarroti's mask ; what then ?
We show the sort of monster Romney is,   520
With godlike virtues and heroic aims
Subjoined to limping possibilities
Of mismade human nature.   Grant the man
Twice godlike, twice heroic, — still he limps,
And here's the point we come to."
                               " Pardon me,
But, Lady Waldemar, the point's the thing
We never come to."
                       " Caustic, insolent
At need !   I like you " — (there, she took my hands)
" And now, my lioness, help Androcles,
For all your roaring.   Help me ! for myself   530
I would not say so — but for him.   He limps
So certainly, he'll fall into the pit
A week hence, — so I lose him — so he is lost !
For when he's fairly married, he a Leigh,
To a girl of doubtful life, undoubtful birth,
Starved out in London till her coarse-grained hands
Are whiter than her morals, — even you
May call his choice unworthy."
                           " Married ! lost !
He . . . Romney ! "

             "Ah, you're moved at last," she said.
"These monsters, set out in the open sun,   540
Of course throw monstrous shadows: those who
    think
Awry, will scarce act straightly.   Who but he?
And who but you can wonder?   He has been mad,
The whole world knows, since first, a nominal man,
He soured the proctors, tried the gownsmen's wits,
With equal scorn of triangles and wine,
And took no honours, yet was honourable.
They'll tell you he lost count of Homer's ships
In Melbourne's poor-bills, Ashley's factory bills, —
Ignored the Aspasia we all dare to praise,   550
For other women, dear, we could not name
Because we're decent.   Well, he had some right
On his side probably; men always have
Who go absurdly wrong.   The living boor
Who brews your ale exceeds in vital worth
Dead Cæsar who 'stops bungholes' in the cask;
And also, to do good is excellent,
For persons of his income, even to boors:
I sympathise with all such things.   But he   559
Went mad upon them . . . madder and more mad
From college times to these, — as, going down hill,
The faster still, the farther.   You must know
Your Leigh by heart: he has sown his black young
    curls
With bleaching cares of half a million men
Already.   If you do not starve, or sin,
You're nothing to him: pay the income-tax
And break your heart upon't, he'll scarce be touched;
But come upon the parish, qualified
For the parish stocks, and Romney will be there
To call you brother, sister, or perhaps   570

A tenderer name still.   Had I any chance
With Mister Leigh, who am Lady Waldemar
And never committed felony ? ''

                                        '' You speak
Too bitterly,'' I said, '' for the literal truth.''

'' The truth is bitter.   Here's a man who looks
For ever on the ground ! you must be low,
Or else a pictured ceiling overhead,
Good painting thrown away.   For me, I've done
What women may — we're somewhat limited,
We modest women — but I've done my best.   580
— How men are perjured when they swear our eyes
Have meaning in them ! they're just blue or brown,
They just can drop their lids a little.   And yet
Mine did more, for I read half Fourier through,
Proudhon, Considérant, and Louis Blanc,
With various others of his socialists,
And, if I had been a fathom less in love,
Had cured myself with gaping.   As it was,
I quoted from them prettily enough,
Perhaps, to make them sound half rational   590
To a saner man than he whene'er we talked
(For which I dodged occasion) — learnt by heart
His speeches in the Commons and elsewhere
Upon the social question ; heaped reports
Of wicked women and penitentiaries
On all my tables (with a place for Sue),
And gave my name to swell subscription lists
Toward keeping up the sun at nights in heaven,
And other possible ends.   All things I did,   599
Except the impossible . . . such as wearing gowns
Provided by the Ten Hours' movement : there
I stopped — we must stop somewhere.   He, meanwhile

Unmoved as the Indian tortoise 'neath the world,
Let all that noise go on upon his back :
He would not disconcert or throw me out,
'Twas well to see a woman of my class
With such a dawn of conscience.   For the heart,
Made firewood for his sake, and flaming up
To his face, — he merely warmed his feet at it :
Just deigned to let my carriage stop him short   610
In park or street, — he leaning on the door
With news of the committee which sat last
On pickpockets at suck."

                  "You jest — you jest."

"As martyrs jest, dear (if you read their lives),
Upon the axe which kills them.   When all's done
By me, . . . for him — you'll ask him presently
The colour of my hair — he cannot tell,
Or answers 'dark' at random ; while, be sure,
He's absolute on the figure, five or ten,
Of my last subscription.   Is it bearable,   620
And I a woman ?"

              "Is it reparable,
Though *I* were a man ?"

                "I know not.   That's to prove.
But, first, this shameful marriage ?"

                    "Ay ?" I cried.
"Then really there's a marriage ?"

                    "Yesterday
I held him fast upon it.   'Mister Leigh,'
Said I, 'shut up a thing, it makes more noise.
'The boiling town keeps secrets ill ; I've known
'Yours since last week.   Forgive my knowledge so :
'You feel I'm not the woman of the world   629
'The world thinks ; you have borne with me before

' And used me in your noble work, our work,
' And now you shall not cast me off because
' You're at the difficult point, the *join.* 'Tis true
' Even I can scarce admit the cogency
' Of such a marriage . . . where you do not love
' (Except the class) yet marry and throw your name
' Down to the gutter, for a fire-escape
' To future generations ! 'tis sublime,
' A great example, a true Genesis
' Of the opening social era. But take heed,   640
' This virtuous act must have a patent weight,
' Or loses half its virtue. Make it tell,
' Interpret it, and set it in the light,
' And do not muffle it in a winter-cloak
' As a vulgar bit of shame,— as if, at best,
' A Leigh had made a misalliance and blushed
' A Howard should know it.' Then, I pressed him
          more :
' He would not choose,' I said, ' that even his
          kin, . . .
' Aurora Leigh, even . . . should conceive his act
' Less sacrifice, more fantasy.' At which   650
He grew so pale, dear, . . . to the lips, I knew
I had touched him. ' Do you know her,' he inquired,
' My cousin Aurora ?' ' Yes,' I said, and lied
(But truly we all know you by your books),
And so I offered to come straight to you,
Explain the subject, justify the cause,
And take you with me to Saint Margaret's Court
To see this miracle, this Marian Erle,
This drover's daughter (she's not pretty, he swears),
Upon whose finger, exquisitely pricked   660
By a hundred needles, we're to hang the tie
'Twixt class and class in England,— thus indeed

By such a presence, yours and mine, to lift
The match up from the doubtful place.   At once
He thanked me sighing, murmured to himself
'She'll do it perhaps, she's noble,'—thanked me
          twice,
And promised, as my guerdon, to put off
His marriage for a month.''
                              I answered then.
'' I understand your drift imperfectly.
You wish to lead me to my cousin's betrothed,   670
To touch her hand if worthy, and hold her hand
If feeble, thus to justify his match.
So be it then.   But how this serves your ends,
And how the strange confession of your love
Serves this, I have to learn — I cannot see.''

She knit her restless forehead.   '' Then, despite,
Aurora, that most radiant morning name,
You're dull as any London afternoon.
I wanted time, and gained it,— wanted *you*,
And gain you ! you will come and see the girl   680
In whose most prodigal eyes the lineal pearl
And pride of all your lofty race of Leighs
Is destined to solution.   Authorised
By sight and knowledge, then, you'll speak your
          mind,
And prove to Romney, in your brilliant way,
He'll wrong the people and posterity
(Say such a thing is bad for me and you,
And you fail utterly), by concluding thus
An execrable marriage.   Break it up,
Disroot it — peradventure presently   690
We'll plant a better fortune in its place.
Be good to me, Aurora, scorn me less

For saying the thing I should not. Well I know
I should not. I have kept, as others have,
The iron rule of womanly reserve
In lip and life, till now : I wept a week
Before I came here."— Ending, she was pale ;
The last words, haughtily said, were tremulous.
This palfrey pranced in harness, arched her neck,
And, only by the foam upon the bit,   700
You saw she champed against it.
                                          Then I rose.
" I love love : truth's no cleaner thing than love.
I comprehend a love so fiery hot
It burns its natural veil of August shame,
And stands sublimely in the nude, as chaste
As Medicean Venus. But I know,
A love that burns through veils will burn through
        masks
And shrivel up treachery. What, love and lie !
Nay — go to the opera ! your love's curable."   709

" I love and lie ? " she said — " I lie, forsooth ? "
And beat her taper foot upon the floor,
And smiled against the shoe,— " You're hard, Miss
        Leigh,
Unversed in current phrases. — Bowling greens
Of poets are fresher than the world's highways :
Forgive me that I rashly blew the dust
Which dims our hedges even, in your eyes,
And vexed you so much. You find, probably,
No evil in this marriage,— rather good
Of innocence, to pastoralise in song :
You'll give the bond your signature, perhaps,   720
Beneath the lady's mark, — indifferent
That Romney chose a wife could write her name,

In witnessing he loved her.''

           '' Loved !'' I cried ;
'' Who tells you that he wants a wife to love ?
He gets a horse to use, not love, I think :
There's work for wives as well,— and after, straw,
When men are liberal.   For myself, you err
Supposing power in me to break this match.
I could not do it to save Romney's life,
And would not to save mine.''

           '' You take it so,'' 730
She said, '' farewell then.   Write your books in peace,
As far as may be for some secret stir
Now obvious to me, — for, most obviously,
In coming hither I mistook the way.''
Whereat she touched my hand and bent her head,
And floated from me like a silent cloud
That leaves the sense of thunder.

           I drew a breath,
Oppressed in my deliverance.   After all,
This woman breaks her social system up
For love, so counted — the love possible   740
To such, — and lilies are still lilies, pulled
By smutty hands, though spotted from their white ;
And thus she is better haply, of her kind,
Than Romney Leigh, who lives by diagrams,
And crosses out the spontaneities
Of all his individual, personal life
With formal universals.   As if man
Were set upon a high stool at a desk
To keep God's books for Him in red and black,
And feel by millions !   What, if even God   750
Were chiefly God by living out Himself
To an individualism of the Infinite,
Eterne, intense, profuse, — still throwing up

The golden spray of multitudinous worlds
In measure to the proclive weight and rush
Of His inner nature, — the spontaneous love
Still proof and outflow of spontaneous life ?
Then live, Aurora.
            Two hours afterward,
Within Saint Margaret's Court I stood alone,
Close-veiled. A sick child, from an ague-fit,   760
Whose wasted right had gambled 'gainst his left
With an old brass button in a blot of sun,
Jeered weakly at me as I passed across
The uneven pavement ; while a woman, rouged
Upon the angular cheek-bones, kerchief torn,
Thin dangling locks, and flat lascivious mouth,
Cursed at a window both ways, in and out,
By turns some bed-rid creature and myself, —
"Lie still there, mother ! liker the dead dog
You'll be to-morrow. What, we pick our way,   770
Fine madam, with those damnable small feet !
We cover up our face from doing good,
As if it were our purse ! What brings you here,
My lady ? Is't to find my gentleman
Who visits his tame pigeon in the eaves ?
Our cholera catch you with its cramps and spasms,
And tumble up your good clothes, veil and all,
And turn your whiteness dead-blue." I looked up ;
I think I could have walked through hell that day,
And never flinched. "The dear Christ comfort
    you,"   780
I said, "you must have been most miserable
To be so cruel," — and I emptied out
My purse upon the stones : when, as I had cast
The last charm in the cauldron, the whole court
Went boiling, bubbling up, from all its doors

And windows, with a hideous wail of laugh
And roar of oaths, and blows perhaps . . . I passed
Too quickly for distinguishing . . . and pushed
A little side-door hanging on a hinge,   789
And plunged into the dark, and groped and climbed
The long, steep, narrow stair 'twixt broken rail
And mildewed wall that let the plaster drop
To startle me in the blackness.   Still, up, up !
So high lived Romney's bride.   I paused at last
Before a low door in the roof, and knocked.
There came an answer like a hurried dove —
" So soon ? can that be Mister Leigh ? so soon ? "
And, as I entered, an ineffable face
Met mine upon the threshold.   " Oh, not you,
Not you ! " — the dropping of the voice implied ; 800
" Then, if not you, for me not any one."
I looked her in the eyes, and held her hands,
And said " I am his cousin, — Romney Leigh's ;
And here I come to see my cousin too."
She touched me with her face and with her voice,
This daughter of the people.   Such soft flowers
From such rough roots ?   The people, under there,
Can sin so, curse so, look so, smell so . . . faugh !
Yet have such daughters ?

                                    Nowise beautiful
Was Marian Erle.   She was not white nor brown, 810
But could look either, like a mist that changed
According to being shone on more or less :
The hair, too, ran its opulence of curls
In doubt 'twixt dark and bright, nor left you clear
To name the colour.   Too much hair perhaps
(I'll name a fault here) for so small a head,
Which seemed to droop on that side and on this,
As a full-blown rose uneasy with its weight

Though not a wind should trouble it.   Again,
The dimple in the cheek had better gone   820
With redder, fuller rounds ; and somewhat large
The mouth was, though the milky little teeth
Dissolved it to so infantine a smile.
For soon it smiled at me ; the eyes smiled too,
But 'twas as if remembering they had wept,
And knowing they should, some day, weep again.

We talked.   She told me all her story out,
Which I'll retell with fuller utterance,
As coloured and confirmed in after times
By others and herself too.   Marian Erle   830
Was born upon the ledge of Malvern Hill,
To eastward, in a hut built up at night,
To evade the landlord's eye, of mud and turf,
Still liable, if once he looked that way,
To being straight levelled, scattered by his foot,
Like any other anthill.   Born, I say ;
God sent her to His world, commissioned right,
Her human testimonials fully signed,
Not scant in soul — complete in lineaments ;
But others had to swindle her a place   840
To wail in when she had come.   No place for her,
By man's law ! born an outlaw was this babe ;
Her first cry in our strange and strangling air,
When cast in spasms out by the shuddering womb.
Was wrong against the social code, — forced wrong : —
What business had the baby to cry there ?

I tell her story and grow passionate.
She, Marian, did not tell it so, but used
Meek words that made no wonder of herself
For being so sad a creature.   " Mister Leigh   850

" Considered truly that such things should change.
" They *will*, in heaven — but meantime, on the
    earth,
" There's none can like a nettle as a pink,
" Except himself. We're nettles, some of us,
" And give offence by the act of springing up ;
" And, if we leave the damp side of the wall,
" The hoes, of course, are on us." So she said.
Her father earned his life by random jobs
Despised by steadier workmen — keeping swine
On commons, picking hops, or hurrying on   860
The harvest at wet seasons, or, at need,
Assisting the Welsh drovers, when a drove
Of startled horses plunged into the mist
Below the mountain-road, and sowed the wind
With wandering neighings. In between the gaps
Of such irregular work he drank and slept,
And cursed his wife because, the pence being out,
She could not buy more drink. At which she turned
(The worm), and beat her baby in revenge
For her own broken heart. There's not a crime 870
But takes its proper change out still in crime
If once rung on the counter of this world :
Let sinners look to it.
                Yet the outcast child,
For whom the very mother's face forwent
The mother's special patience, lived and grew ;
Learnt early to cry low, and walk alone,
With that pathetic vacillating roll
Of the infant body on the uncertain feet
(The earth being felt unstable ground so soon),
At which most women's arms unclose at once 880
With irrepressive instinct. Thus, at three,
This poor weaned kid would run off from the fold,

This babe would steal off from the mother's chair,
And, creeping through the golden walls of gorse,
Would find some keyhole toward the secrecy
Of Heaven's high blue, and, nestling down, peer out —
Oh, not to catch the angels at their games, —
She had never heard of angels, — but to gaze
She knew not why, to see she knew not what,
A-hungering outward from the barren earth   890
For something like a joy.   She liked, she said,
To dazzle black her sight against the sky,
For then, it seemed, some grand blind Love came down,
And groped her out, and clasped her with a kiss ;
She learnt God that way, and was beat for it
Whenever she went home, — yet came again,
As surely as the trapped hare, getting free,
Returns to his form.   This grand blind Love, she
        said,
This skyey father and mother both in one,
Instructed her and civilised her more   900
Than even Sunday-school did afterward,
To which a lady sent her to learn books
And sit upon a long bench in a row
With other children.   Well, she laughed sometimes
To see them laugh and laugh and maul their texts ;
But ofter she was sorrowful with noise
And wondered if their mothers beat them hard
That ever they should laugh so.   There was one
She loved indeed, — Rose Bell, a seven years' child,
So pretty and clever, who read syllables   910
When Marian was at letters ; *she* would laugh
At nothing — hold your finger up, she laughed,
Then shook her curls down over eyes and mouth
To hide her make-mirth from the school-master :
And Rose's pelting glee, as frank as rain

On cherry-blossoms, brightened Marian too,
To see another merry whom she loved.
She whispered once (the children side by side,
With mutual arms entwined about their necks)
"Your mother lets you laugh so?" "Ay," said
    Rose.   920
"She lets me.   She was dug into the ground
Six years since, I being but a yearling wean.
Such mothers let us play and lose our time,
And never scold nor beat us !   Don't you wish
You had one like that?"   There, Marian breaking off
Looked suddenly in my face.   "Poor Rose," said
    she,
"I heard her laugh last night in Oxford Street.
I'd pour out half my blood to stop that laugh.   928
Poor Rose, poor Rose !" said Marian.

                                        She resumed.
It tried her, when she had learnt at Sunday-school
What God was, what he wanted from us all,
And how in choosing sin we vexed the Christ,
To go straight home and hear her father pull
The Name down on us from the thunder-shelf,
Then drink away his soul into the dark
From seeing judgment.   Father, mother, home,
Were God and heaven reversed to her : the more
She knew of Right, the more she guessed their wrong :
Her price paid down for knowledge, was to know
The vileness of her kindred : through her heart,   940
Her filial and tormented heart, henceforth,
They struck their blows at virtue.   Oh, 'tis hard
To learn you have a father up in heaven
By a gathering certain sense of being, on earth,
Still worse than orphaned : 'tis too heavy a grief,
The having to thank God for such a joy !

And so passed Marian's life from year to year.
Her parents took her with them when they tramped,
Dodged lanes and heaths, frequented towns and fairs,
And once went farther and saw Manchester, 950
And once the sea, that blue end of the world,
That fair scroll-finis of a wicked book, —
And twice a prison, — back at intervals,
Returning to the hills. Hills draw like heaven,
And stronger sometimes, holding out their hands
To pull you from the vile flats up to them.
And though perhaps these strollers still strolled back,
As sheep do, simply that they knew the way,
They certainly felt bettered unaware
Emerging from the social smut of towns 960
To wipe their feet clean on the mountain turf.
In which long wanderings, Marian lived and learned,
Endured and learned. The people on the roads
Would stop and ask her why her eyes outgrew
Her cheeks, and if she meant to lodge the birds
In all that hair ; and then they lifted her,
The miller in his cart, a mile or twain,
The butcher's boy on horseback. Often too
The pedlar stopped, and tapped her on the head
With absolute forefinger, brown and ringed, 970
And asked if peradventure she could read,
And when she answered " ay," would toss her down
Some stray odd volume from his heavy pack,
A Thomson's Seasons, mulcted of the Spring,
Or half a play of Shakespeare's, torn across
(She had to guess the bottom of a page
By just the top sometimes, — as difficult,
As, sitting on the moon, to guess the earth !),
Or else a sheaf of leaves (for that small Ruth's 979
Small gleanings) torn out from the heart of books,

From Churchyard Elegies and Edens Lost,
From Burns, and Bunyan, Selkirk, and Tom Jones, —
'Twas somewhat hard to keep the things distinct,
And oft the jangling influence jarred the child
Like looking at a sunset full of grace
Through a pothouse window while the drunken oaths
Went on behind her.   But she weeded out
Her book-leaves, threw away the leaves that hurt
(First tore them small, that none should find a word),
And made a nosegay of the sweet and good   990
To fold within her breast, and pore upon
At broken moments of the noontide glare,
When leave was given her to untie her cloak
And rest upon the dusty highway's bank
From the road's dust : or oft, the journey done,
Some city friend would lead her by the hand
To hear a lecture at an institute.
And thus she had grown, this Marian Erle of ours,
To no book-learning, — she was ignorant
Of authors, — not in earshot of the things   1000
Outspoken o'er the heads of common men
By men who are uncommon, — but within
The cadenced hum of such, and capable
Of catching from the fringes of the wing
Some fragmentary phrases, here and there,
Of that fine music, — which, being carried in
To her soul, had reproduced itself afresh
In finer motions of the lips and lids.

She said, in speaking of it, " If a flower
Were thrown you out of heaven at intervals,   1010
You'd soon attain to a trick of looking up, —
And so with her."   She counted me her years,
Till *I* felt old ; and then she counted me

Her sorrowful pleasures, till I felt ashamed.
She told me she was fortunate and calm
On such and such a season, sat and sewed,
With no one to break up her crystal thoughts,
While rhymes from lovely poems span around
Their ringing circles of estatic tune,
Beneath the moistened finger of the Hour.   1020
Her parents called her a strange, sickly child,
Not good for much, and given to sulk and stare,
And smile into the hedges and the clouds,
And tremble if one shook her from her fit
By any blow, or word even.   Out-door jobs
Went ill with her, and household quiet work
She was not born to.   Had they kept the north,
They might have had their pennyworth out of her,
Like other parents, in the factories   1029
(Your children work for you, not you for them,
Or else they better had been choked with air
The first breath drawn) ; but, in this tramping life,
Was nothing to be done with such a child
But tramp and tramp.   And yet she knitted hose
Not ill, and was not dull at needlework ;
And all the country people gave her pence
For darning stockings past their natural age,
And patching petticoats from old to new,
And other light work done for thrifty wives.   1039

One day, said Marian — the sun shone that day —
Her mother had been badly beat, and felt
The bruises sore about her wretched soul
(That must have been) : she came in suddenly,
And snatching in a sort of breathless rage
Her daughter's headgear comb, let down the hair
Upon her like a sudden waterfall,

Then drew her drenched and passive by the arm
Outside the hut they lived in.   When the child
Could clear her blinded face from all that stream
Of tresses . . . there, a man stood, with beast's
        eyes   1050
That seemed as they would swallow her alive
Complete in body and spirit, hair and all, —
And burning stertorous breath that hurt her cheek,
He breathed so near.   The mother held her tight,
Saying hard between her teeth — " Why wench,
        why wench,
The squire speaks to you now — the squire's too
        good :
He means to set you up, and comfort us.
Be mannerly at least."   The child turned round
And looked up piteous in the mother's face
(Be sure that mother's death-bed will not want   1060
Another devil to damn, than such a look),
" Oh, mother ! " then, with desperate glance to
        heaven,
" God, free me from my mother," she shrieked out,
" These mothers are too dreadful."   And, with
        force
As passionate as fear, she tore her hands,
Like lilies from the rocks, from hers and his,
And sprang down, bounded headlong down the steep,
Away from both — away, if possible,
As far as God, — away !   They yelled at her,
As famished hounds at a hare.   She heard them
        yell ;   1070
She felt her name hiss after her from the hills,
Like shot from guns.   On, on.   And now she had
        cast
The voices off with the uplands.   On.   Mad fear

Was running in her feet and killing the ground ;
The white roads curled as if she burnt them up,
The green fields melted, wayside trees fell back
To make room for her.   Then her head grew vexed ;
Trees, fields, turned on her and ran after her ;
She heard the quick pants of the hills behind,   1079
Their keen air pricked her neck : she had lost her feet,
Could run no more, yet somehow went as fast,
The horizon red 'twixt steeples in the east
So sucked her forward, forward, while her heart
Kept swelling, swelling, till it swelled so big
It seemed to fill her body, — when it burst
And overflowed the world and swamped the light ;
"And now I am dead and safe," thought Marian
    Erle —
She had dropped, she had fainted.

                    As the sense returned,
The night had passed — not life's night.   She was
    'ware
Of heavy tumbling motions, creaking wheels,   1090
The driver shouting to the lazy team
That swung their rankling bells against her brain,
While, through the waggon's coverture and chinks,
The cruel yellow morning pecked at her
Alive or dead upon the straw inside,—
At which her soul ached back into the dark
And prayed, "no more of that."   A waggoner
Had found her in a ditch beneath the moon,
As white as moonshine save for the oozing blood.
At first he thought her dead ; but when he had
    wiped   1100
The mouth and heard it sigh, he raised her up,
And laid her in his waggon in the straw,
And so conveyed her to the distant town

To which his business called himself, and left
That heap of misery at the hospital.

She stirred ; — the place seemed new and strange as
    death.
The white strait bed, with others strait and white,
Like graves dug side by side at measured lengths,
And quiet people walking in and out
With wonderful low voices and soft steps   1110
And apparitional equal care for each,
Astonished her with order, silence, law.
And when a gentle hand held out a cup,
She took it, as you do at sacrament,
Half awed, half melted, — not being used, indeed,
To so much love as makes the form of love
And courtesy of manners.   Delicate drinks
And rare white bread, to which some dying eyes
Were turned in observation.   O my God,
How sick we must be, ere we make men just !   1120
I think it frets the saints in heaven to see
How many desolate creatures on the earth
Have learnt the simple dues of fellowship
And social comfort, in a hospital,
As Marian did.   She lay there, stunned, half tranced,
And wished, at intervals of growing sense,
She might be sicker yet, if sickness made
The world so marvellous kind, the air so hushed,
And all her wake-time quiet as a sleep ;
For now she understood (as such things were)   1130
How sickness ended very oft in heaven
Among the unspoken raptures : — yet more sick,
And surelier happy.   Then she dropped her lids,
And, folding up her hands as flowers at night,
Would lose no moment of the blessed time.

She lay and seethed in fever many weeks,
But youth was strong and overcame the test;
Revolted soul and flesh were reconciled
And fetched back to the necessary day
And daylight duties. She could creep about   1140
The long bare rooms, and stare out drearily
From any narrow window on the street,
Till some one who had nursed her as a friend
Said coldly to her, as an enemy,
" She had leave to go next week, being well enough,"
(While only her heart ached). " Go next week,"
   thought she :
" Next week ! how would it be with her next week,
Let out into that terrible street alone
Among the pushing people, . . . to go . . . where ? "

One day, the last before the dreaded last,   1150
Among the convalescents, like herself
Prepared to go next morning, she sat dumb,
And heard half absently the women talk, —
How one was famished for her baby's cheeks,
" The little wretch would know her ! a year old
And lively, like his father ! " — one was keen
To get to work, and fill some clamorous mouths ;
And one was tender for her dear goodman
Who had missed her sorely, — and one, querulous . . .
" Would pay backbiting neighbours who had dared
To talk about her as already dead," —   1161
And one was proud . . . " and if her sweetheart
   Luke
Had left her for a ruddier face than hers
(The gossip would be seen through at a glance),
Sweet riddance of such sweethearts — let him hang !
'Twere good to have been sick for such an end."

And while they talked, and Marian felt the worse
For having missed the worst of all their wrongs,
A visitor was ushered through the wards   1169
And paused among the talkers. "When he looked
It was as if he spoke, and when he spoke
He sang perhaps," said Marian ; "could she tell ?
She only knew " (so much she had chronicled,
As seraphs might the making of the sun)
"That he who came and spake was Romney Leigh,
And then and there she saw and heard him first."

And when it was her turn to have the face
Upon her, all those buzzing pallid lips
Being satisfied with comfort — when he changed
To   Marian,   saying " And *you ?* you're going,
      where ? " —   1180
She, moveless as a worm beneath a stone
Which some one's stumbling foot has spurned aside,
Writhed suddenly, astonished with the light,
And, breaking into sobs, cried " Where I go ?
None asked me till this moment.   Can I say
Where *I* go, — when it has not seemed worth while
To God Himself, who thinks of every one,
To think of me and fix where I shall go ? "

" So young," he gently asked her, " you have lost
Your father and your mother ? "

                              " Both," she said, 1190
" Both lost ! my father was burnt up with gin
Or ever I sucked milk, and so is lost.
My mother sold me to a man last month,
And so my mother's lost, 'tis manifest.
And I, who fled from her for miles and miles,
As if I had caught sight of the fire of hell

Through some wild gap (she was my mother, sir),
It seems I shall be lost too, presently,
And so we end, all three of us."

           " Poor child,"
He said, — with such a pity in his voice,   1200
It soothed her more than her own tears, — "poor
    child !
'Tis simple that betrayal by mother's love
Should bring despair of God's too.   Yet be taught,
He's better to us than many mothers are,
And children cannot wander beyond reach
Of the sweep of his white raiment. Touch and hold !
And if you weep still, weep where John was laid
While Jesus loved him."

          " She could say the words,"
She told me, " exactly as he uttered them
A year back, since in any doubt or dark   1210
They came out like the stars, and shone on her
With just their comfort.   Common words, perhaps ;
The ministers in church might say the same ;
But *he*, he made the church with what he spoke, —
The difference was the miracle," said she.

Then catching up her smile to ravishment,
She added quickly, " I repeat his words,
But not his tones : can any one repeat
The music of an organ, out of church ?   1219
And when he said ' poor child,' I shut my eyes
To feel how tenderly his voice broke through,
As the ointment-box broke on the Holy feet
To let out the rich medicative nard."

She told me how he had raised and rescued her
With reverent pity, as, in touching grief,

He touched the wounds of Christ, — and made her
    feel
More self-respecting.   Hope he called belief
In God, — work, worship, — therefore let us pray !
And thus, to snatch her soul from atheism,
And keep it stainless from her mother's face,   1230
He sent her to a famous sempstress-house
Far off in London, there to work and hope.

With that, they parted.   She kept sight of Heaven,
But not of Romney.   He had good to do
To others : through the days and through the nights
She sewed and sewed and sewed.   She drooped some-
    times,
And wondered, while along the tawny light
She struck the new thread into her needle's eye,
How people without mothers on the hills   1239
Could choose the town to live in ! — then she drew
The stitch, and mused how Romney's face would
    look,
And if 'twere likely he'd remember hers
When they two had their meeting after death.

FOURTH BOOK.

THEY met still sooner.   'Twas a year from thence
That Lucy Gresham, the sick sempstress girl,
Who sewed by Marian's chair so still and quick,
And leant her head upon its back to cough
More freely, when, the mistress turning round,
The others took occasion to laugh out,
Gave up at last.   Among the workers, spoke
A bold girl with black eyebrows and red lips :

" You know the news ?   Who's dying, do you
    think ?
Our Lucy Gresham.   I expected it   10
As little as Nell Hart's wedding.   Blush not, Nell,
Thy curls be red enough without thy cheeks,
And, some day, there'll be found a man to dote
On red curls. — Lucy Gresham swooned last night,
Dropped sudden in the street while going home ;
And now the baker says, who took her up
And laid her by her grandmother in bed,
He'll give her a week to die in.   Pass the silk.
Let's hope he gave her a loaf too, within reach,
For otherwise they'll starve before they die,   20
That funny pair of bedfellows !   Miss Bell,
I'll thank you for the scissors.   The old crone
Is paralytic — that's the reason why
Our Lucy's thread went faster than her breath,
Which went too quick, we all know.   Marian Erle,
Why, Marian Erle, you're not the fool to cry ?
Your tears spoil Lady Waldemar's new dress,
You piece of pity ! ' "
                Marian rose up straight,
And, breaking through the talk and through the work,
Went outward, in the face of their surprise,   30
To Lucy's home, to nurse her back to life
Or down to death.   She knew, by such an act,
All place and grace were forfeit in the house,
Whose mistress would supply the missing hand
With necessary, not inhuman haste,
And take no blame.   But pity, too, had dues :
She could not leave a solitary soul
To founder in the dark, while she sat still
And lavished stitches on a lady's hem
As if no other work were paramount.   40

"Why, God," thought Marian, "has a missing
    hand
This moment; Lucy wants a drink, perhaps.
Let others miss me! never miss me, God!"

So Marian sat by Lucy's bed, content
With duty, and was strong, for recompense,
To hold the lamp of human love arm-high,
To catch the death-strained eyes and comfort them,
Until the angels, on the luminous side
Of death, had got theirs ready.   And she said,
If Lucy thanked her sometimes, called her kind,   50
It touched her strangely.   "Marian Erle called kind!
What, Marian, beaten and sold, who could not die!
'Tis verily good fortune to be kind.
Ah you," she said, "who are born to such a grace,
Be sorry for the unlicensed class, the poor,
Reduced to think the best good fortune means
That others, simply, should be kind to them."

From sleep to sleep when Lucy had slid away
So gently, like the light upon a hill,
Of which none names the moment that it goes   60
Though all see when 'tis gone, — a man came in
And stood beside the bed.   The old idiot wretch
Screamed feebly, like a baby overlain,
"Sir, sir, you won't mistake me for the corpse?
Don't look at *me*, sir! never bury *me*!
Although I lie here, I'm alive as you,
Except my legs and arms, — I eat and drink
And understand, — (that you're the gentleman
Who fits the funerals up, Heaven speed you, sir),
And certainly I should be livelier still   70
If Lucy here . . . sir, Lucy is the corpse . . .

Had worked more properly to buy me wine ;
But Lucy, sir, was always slow at work,
I shan't lose much by Lucy.   Marian Erle,
Speak up and show the gentleman the corpse.''

And a voice said '' Marian Erle.''   She rose ;
It was the hour for angels — there, stood hers !
She scarcely marvelled to see Romney Leigh.
As light November snows to empty nests,
As grass to graves, as moss to mildewed stones,   80
As July suns to ruins, through the rents,
As ministering spirits to mourners, through a loss,
As Heaven itself to men, through pangs of death,
He came uncalled wherever grief had come.
'' And so,'' said Marian Erle, '' we met anew,''
And added softly, '' so, we shall not part.''

He was not angry that she had left the house
Wherein he placed her.   Well — she had feared it might
Have vexed him.   Also, when he found her set
On keeping, though the dead was out of sight,   90
That half-dead, half-alive body left behind
With cankerous heart and flesh, which took your best
And cursed you for the little good it did
(Could any leave the bed-rid wretch alone,
So joyless she was thankless even to God,
Much more to you ?), he did not say 'twas well,
Yet Marian thought he did not take it ill, —
Since day by day he came, and every day
She felt within his utterance and his eyes
A closer, tenderer presence of the soul,   100
Until at last he said '' We shall not part.''

On that same day was Marian's work complete :
She had smoothed the empty bed, and swept the floor
Of coffin sawdust, set the chairs anew
The dead had ended gossip in, and stood
In that poor room so cold and orderly,
The door-key in her hand, prepared to go
As *they* had, howbeit not their way.   He spoke.

" Dear Marian, of one clay God made us all,
And though men push and poke and paddle in't   110
(As children play at fashioning dirt-pies)
And call their fancies by the name of facts,
Assuming difference, lordship, privilege,
When all's plain dirt, — they come back to it at last,
The first grave-digger proves it with a spade,
And pats all even.   Need we wait for this,
You, Marian, and I, Romney ? ''

                    She, at that,
Looked blindly in his face, as when one looks
Through driving autumn-rains to find the sky.
He went on speaking.   " Marian, I being born   120
What men call noble, and you, issued from
The noble people, — though the tyrannous sword,
Which pierced Christ's heart, has cleft the world in
      twain
'Twixt class and class, opposing rich to poor,
Shall *we* keep parted ?   Not so.   Let us lean
And strain together rather, each to each,
Compress the red lips of this gaping wound
As far as two souls can, — ay, lean and league,
I from my superabundance, — from your want
You, — joining in a protest 'gainst the wrong   130
On both sides.''

               All the rest, he held her hand

In speaking, which confused the sense of much.
Her heart against his words beat out so thick,
They might as well be written on the dust
Where some poor bird, escaping from hawk's beak,
Has dropped and beats its shuddering wings, — the
    lines
Are rubbed so, — yet 'twas something like to this,
— " That they two, standing at the two extremes
Of social classes, had received one seal,
Been dedicate and drawn beyond themselves   140
To mercy and ministration, — he, indeed,
Through what he knew, and she, through what she
    felt,
He, by man's conscience, she, by woman's heart,
Relinquishing their several 'vantage posts
Of wealthy ease and honourable toil,
To work with God at love.   And since God willed
That putting out his hand to touch this ark
He found a woman's hand there, he'd accept
The sign too, hold the tender fingers fast,
And say ' My fellow-worker, be my wife ! ' "   150

She told the tale with simple, rustic turns, —
Strong leaps of meaning in her sudden eyes
That took the gaps of any imperfect phrase
Of the unschooled speaker : I have rather writ
The thing I understood so, than the thing
I heard so.   And I cannot render right
Her quick gesticulation, wild yet soft,
Self-startled from the habitual mood she used,
Half sad, half languid, — like dumb creatures (now
A rustling bird, and now a wandering deer,   160
Or squirrel 'gainst the oak-gloom flashing up
His sidelong burnished head, in just her way

Of savage spontaneity), that stir
Abruptly the green silence of the woods,
And make it stranger, holier, more profound ;
As Nature's general heart confessed itself
Of life, and then fell backward on repose.

I kissed the lips that ended. — " So indeed
He loves you, Marian ? "

                              " Loves me ! "   She looked up
With a child's wonder when you ask him first   170
Who made the sun — a puzzled blush, that grew,
Then broke off in a rapid radiant smile
Of sure solution.   " Loves me ! he loves all, —
And me, of course.   He had not asked me else
To work with him for ever and be his wife."

Her words reproved me.   This perhaps was love —
To have its hands too full of gifts to give,
For putting out a hand to take a gift ;
To love so much, the perfect round of love
Includes, in strict conclusion, being loved ;   180
As Eden-dew went up and fell again,
Enough for watering Eden.   Obviously
She had not thought about his love at all :
The cataracts of her soul had poured themselves,
And risen self-crowned in rainbow : would she ask
Who crowned her ? — it sufficed that she was
      crowned.
With women of my class 'tis otherwise :
We haggle for the small change of our gold,
And so much love accord for so much love,
Rialto-prices.   Are we therefore wrong ?   190
If marriage be a contract, look to it then,
Contracting parties should be equal, just ;

But if, a simple fealty on one side,
A mere religion, — right to give, is all,
And certain brides of Europe duly ask
To mount the pile as Indian widows do,
The spices of their tender youth heaped up,
The jewels of their gracious virtues worn,
More gems, more glory, — to consume entire
For a living husband : as the man's alive,   200
Not dead, the woman's duty by so much
Advanced in England beyond Hindostan.

I sat there musing, till she touched my hand
With hers, as softly as a strange white bird
She feared to startle in touching. "You are kind,
But are you, peradventure, vexed at heart
Because your cousin takes me for a wife ?
I know I am not worthy — nay, in truth,
I'm glad on't, since, for that, he chooses me.
He likes the poor things of the world the best ;   210
I would not therefore, if I could, be rich.
It pleasures him to stoop for buttercups ;
I would not be a rose upon the wall
A queen might stop at, near the palace-door,
To say to a courtier ' Pluck that rose for me,
' It's prettier than the rest.'   O Romney Leigh !
I'd rather far be trodden by his foot,
Than lie in a great queen's bosom."

                        Out of breath,
She paused.
            "Sweet Marian, do you disavow
The roses with that face ? "
                  She dropped her head 220
As if the wind had caught that flower of her
And bent it in the garden, — then looked up

With grave assurance.   " Well, you think me bold !
But so we all are, when we're praying God.
And if I'm bold — yet, lady, credit me,
That, since I know myself for what I am,
Much fitter for his handmaid than his wife,
I'll prove the handmaid and the wife at once,
Serve tenderly, and love obediently,
And be a worthier mate, perhaps, than some   230
Who are wooed in silk among their learned books ;
While I shall set myself to read his eyes,
Till such grow plainer to me than the French
To wisest ladies.   Do you think I'll miss
A letter, in the spelling of his mind ?
No more than they do when they sit and write
Their flying words with flickering wild-fowl tails,
Nor ever pause to ask how many *t*'s,
Should that be *y* or *i*, they know't so well :
I've seen them writing, when I brought a dress   240
And waited, — floating out their soft white hands
On shining paper.   But they're hard, sometimes,
For all those hands ! — we've used out many nights,
And worn the yellow daylight into shreds
Which flapped and shivered down our aching eyes
Till night appeared more tolerable, just
That pretty ladies might look beautiful,
Who said at last . . . ' You're lazy in that house !
' You're slow in sending home the work, — I count
' I've waited near an hour for't.'   Pardon me,   250
I do not blame them, madam, nor misprize ;
They are fair and gracious ; ay, but not like you,
Since none but you has Mister Leigh's own blood,
Both noble and gentle, — and, without it . . . well,
They are fair, I said ; so fair, it scarce seems strange
That, flashing out in any looking-glass

The wonder of their glorious brows and breasts,
They're charmed so, they forget to look behind
And mark how pale we've grown, we pitiful
Remainders of the world.   And so perhaps   260
If Mister Leigh had chosen a wife from these,
She might, although he's better than her best
And dearly she would know it, steal a thought
Which should be all his, an eye-glance from his face,
To plunge into the mirror opposite
In search of her own beauty's pearl ; while *I* . . .
Ah, dearest lady, serge will outweigh silk
For winter-wear when bodies feel a-cold,
And I'll be a true wife to your cousin Leigh.''

Before I answered he was there himself.   270
I think he had been standing in the room
And listened probably to half her talk,
Arrested, turned to stone, — as white as stone.
Will tender sayings make men look so white ?
He loves her then profoundly.

                              '' You are here,
Aurora ?   Here I meet you ! '' — We clasped hands.

'' Even so, dear Romney.   Lady Waldemar
Has sent me in haste to find a cousin of mine
Who shall be.''

                    '' Lady Waldemar is good.''

'' Here's one, at least, who is good,'' I sighed, and
          touched   280
Poor Marian's happy head, as doglike she,
Most passionately patient, waited on,
A-tremble for her turn of greeting words ;
'' I've sat a full hour with your Marian Erle,

And learnt the thing by heart, — and from my heart
Am therefore competent to give you thanks
For such a cousin."

              " You accept at last
A gift from me, Aurora, without scorn ?
At last I please you ?"— How his voice was changed.

"You cannot please a woman against her will,   290
And once you vexed me.   Shall we speak of that ?
We'll say, then, you were noble in it all,
And I not ignorant — let it pass !   And now
You please me, Romney, when you please yourself ;
So, please you, be fanatical in love,
And I'm well pleased.   Ah, cousin ! at the old hall,
Among the gallery portraits of our Leighs,
We shall not find a sweeter signory
Than this pure forehead's."

                  Not a word he said.
How arrogant men are ! — Even philanthropists, 300
Who try to take a wife up in the way
They put down a subscription-cheque,— if once
She turns and says " I will not tax you so,
Most charitable sir," — feel ill at ease
As though she had wronged them somehow.   I sup-
    pose
We women should remember what we are,
And not throw back an obolus inscribed
With Cæsar's image, lightly.   I resumed.

"It strikes me, some of those sublime Vandykes 309
Were not too proud to make good saints in heaven ;
And if so, then they're not too proud to-day,
To bow down (now the ruffs are off their necks)
And own this good, true, noble Marian, yours,

And mine, I'll say ! — For poets (bear the word),
Half-poets even, are still whole democrats, —
Oh, not that we're disloyal to the high,
But loyal to the low, and cognisant
Of the less scrutable majesties.   For me,
I comprehend your choice, I justify
Your right in choosing."

        " No, no, no," he sighed,   320
With a sort of melancholy, impatient scorn,
As some grown man who never had a child
Puts by some child who plays at being a man,
" You did not, do not, cannot comprehend
My choice, my ends, my motives, nor myself :
No matter now ; we'll let it pass, you say.
I thank you for your generous cousinship
Which helps this present ; I accept for her
Your favourable thoughts.   We're fallen on days,
We two who are not poets, when to wed   330
Requires less mutual love than common love
For two together to bear out at once
Upon the loveless many.   Work in pairs,
In galley-couplings or in marriage-rings,
The difference lies in the honour, not the work, —
And such we're bound to, I and she.   But love
(You poets are benighted in this age,
The hour's too late for catching even moths,
You've gnats instead), love ! — love's fool-paradise
Is out of date, like Adam's.   Set a swan   340
To swim the Trenton, rather than true love
To float its fabulous plumage safely down
The cataracts of this loud transition-time, —
Whose roar for ever henceforth in my ears
Must keep me deaf to music."

        There, I turned

And kissed poor Marian, out of discontent.
The man had baffled, chafed me, till I flung
For refuge to the woman, — as, sometimes,
Impatient of some crowded room's close smell,
You throw a window open and lean out   350
To breathe a long breath in the dewy night
And cool your angry forehead.   She, at least,
Was not built up as walls are, brick by brick,
Each fancy squared, each feeling ranged by line,
The very heat of burning youth applied
To indurate form and system ! excellent bricks,
A well-built wall, — which stops you on the road,
And into which you cannot see an inch
Although you beat your head against it — pshaw !

" Adieu," I said, " for this time, cousins both,   360
And, cousin Romney, pardon me the word,
Be happy ! — oh, in some esoteric sense
Of course ! — I mean no harm in wishing well.
Adieu, my Marian : — may she come to me,
Dear Romney, and be married from my house ?
It is not part of your philosophy
To keep your bird upon the blackthorn ?"
                                        " Ay,"
He answered, " but it is.   I take my wife
Directly from the people, — and she comes,
As Austria's daughter to imperial France,   370
Betwixt her eagles, blinking not her race,
From Margaret's Court at garret-height, to meet
And wed me at Saint James's, nor put off
Her gown of serge for that.   The things we do,
We do : we'll wear no mask, as if we blushed."
" Dear Romney, you're the poet," I replied,
But felt my smile too mournful for my word,

And turned and went.   Ay, masks, I thought, —
    beware
Of tragic masks we tie before the glass,
Uplifted on the cothurn half a yard   380
Above the natural stature ! we would play
Heroic parts to ourselves, — and end, perhaps,
As impotently as Athenian wives
Who shrieked in fits at the Eumenides.

His foot pursued me down the stair.   " At least
You'll suffer me to walk with you beyond
These hideous streets, these graves, where men alive
Packed close with earthworms, burr unconsciously
About the plague that slew them ; let me go,
The very women pelt their souls in mud   390
At any woman who walks here alone.
How came you here alone ? — you are ignorant."

We had a strange and melancholy walk :
The night came drizzling downward in dark rain,
And, as we walked, the colour of the time,
The act, the presence, my hand upon his arm,
His voice in my ear, and mine to my own sense,
Appeared unnatural.   We talked modern books
And daily papers, Spanish marriage-schemes
And English climate — was't so cold last year ?   400
And will the wind change by to-morrow morn ?
Can Guizot stand ? is London full ? is trade
Competitive ? has Dickens turned his hinge
A-pinch upon the fingers of the great ?
And are potatoes to grow mythical
Like moly ? will the apple die out too ?
Which way is the wind to-night ? south-east ? due
    east ?

We talked on fast, while every common word
Seemed tangled with the thunder at one end,
And ready to pull down upon our head   410
A terror out of sight.   And yet to pause
Were surelier mortal : we tore greedily up
All silence, all the innocent breathing-points,
As if, like pale conspirators in haste,
We tore up papers where our signatures
Imperilled us to an ugly shame or death.

I cannot tell you why it was.   'Tis plain
We had not loved nor hated : wherefore dread
To spill gunpowder on ground safe from fire ?
Perhaps we had lived too closely, to diverge   420
So absolutely : leave two clocks, they say,
Wound up to different hours, upon one shelf,
And slowly, through the interior wheels of each,
The blind mechanic motion sets itself
A-throb to feel out for the mutual time.
It was not so with us, indeed : while he
Struck midnight, I kept striking six at dawn ;
While he marked judgment, I, redemption-day ;
And such exception to a general law
Imperious upon inert matter even,   430
Might make us, each to either, insecure,
A beckoning mystery or a troubling fear.

I mind me, when we parted at the door,
How strange his good-night sounded, —like good-
      night
Beside a deathbed, where the morrow's sun
Is sure to come too late for more good-days :
And all that night I thought . . . " Good-night,"
      said he.

And so, a month passed. Let me set it down
At once, — I have been wrong, I have been wrong.
We are wrong always when we think too much 440
Of what we think or are : albeit our thoughts
Be verily bitter as self-sacrifice,
We're no less selfish. If we sleep on rocks
Or roses, sleeping past the hour of noon
We're lazy. This I write against myself.
I had done a duty in the visit paid
To Marian, and was ready otherwise
To give the witness of my presence and name
Whenever she should marry. — Which, I thought,
Sufficed. I even had cast into the scale 450
An overweight of justice toward the match ;
The Lady Waldemar had missed her tool,
Had broken it in the lock as being too straight
For a crooked purpose, while poor Marian Erle
Missed nothing in my accents or my acts :
I had not been ungenerous on the whole,
Nor yet untender ; so, enough. I felt
Tired, overworked : this marriage somewhat jarred ;
Or, if it did not, all the bridal noise,
The pricking of the map of life with pins, 460
In schemes of . . . " Here we'll go," and " There
        we'll stay,"
And " Everywhere we'll prosper in our love,"
Was scarce my business : let them order it ;
Who else should care ? I threw myself aside,
As one who had done her work and shuts her eyes
To rest the better.

            I, who should have known,
Forereckoned mischief ! Where we disavow
Being a keeper to our brother, we're his Cain.

I might have held that poor child to my heart
A little longer ! 'twould have hurt me much   470
To have hastened by its beats the marriage day,
And kept her safe meantime from tampering hands
Or, peradventure, traps.   What drew me back
From telling Romney plainly the designs
Of Lady Waldemar, as spoken out
To me . . . me ?   Had I any right, ay, right,
With womanly compassion and reserve,
To break the fall of woman's impudence ? —
To stand by calmly, knowing what I knew,
And hear him call her *good ?*

                     Distrust that word. 480
" There is none good save God," said Jesus Christ.
If He once, in the first creation-week,
Called creatures good, — for ever, afterward,
The Devil only has done it, and his heirs,
The knaves who win so, and the fools who lose ;
The word's grown dangerous.   In the middle age,
I think they called malignant fays and imps
Good people.   A good neighbour, even in this,
Is fatal sometimes, — cuts your morning up
To mincemeat of the very smallest talk,   490
Then helps to sugar her bohea at night
With your reputation.   I have known good wives,
As chaste, or nearly so, as Potiphar's ;
And good, good mothers, who would use a child
To better an intrigue ; good friends, beside
(Very good), who hung succinctly round your neck
And sucked your breath, as cats are fabled to do
By sleeping infants.   And we all have known
Good critics who have stamped out poet's hope,
Good statesmen who pulled ruin on the state,   500
Good patriots who for a theory risked a cause,

Good kings who disembowelled for a tax,
Good popes who brought all good to jeopardy,
Good Christians who sat still in easy chairs
And damned the general world for standing up. —
Now may the good God pardon all good men !

How bitterly I speak, — how certainly
The innocent white milk in us is turned,
By much persistent shining of the sun ! —
Shake up the sweetest in us long enough,   510
With men, it drops to foolish curd, too sour
To feed the most untender of Christ's lambs.

I should have thought, — a woman of the world
Like her I'm meaning, centre to herself,
Who has wheeled on her own pivot half a life
In isolated self-love and self-will,
As a windmill seen at distance radiating
Its delicate white vans against the sky,
So soft and soundless, simply beautiful,
Seen nearer, — what a roar and tear it makes,   520
How it grinds and bruises ! — if she loves at last,
Her love's a re-adjustment of self-love,
No more, — a need felt of another's use
To her one advantage, as the mill wants grain,
The fire wants fuel, the very wolf wants prey,
And none of these is more unscrupulous
Than such a charming woman when she loves.
She'll not be thwarted by an obstacle
So trifling as . . . her soul is, . . . much less
        yours ! —
Is God a consideration ? — she loves you,   530
Not God ; she will not flinch for Him indeed :
She did not for the Marchioness of Perth,

When wanting tickets for the fancy ball.
She loves you, sir, with passion, to lunacy ;
She loves you like her diamonds . . . almost.

                                                   Well,
A month passed so, and then the notice came,
On such a day the marriage at the church.
I was not backward.

                         Half Saint Giles in frieze
Was bidden to meet Saint James in cloth of gold,
And, after contract at the altar, pass   540
To eat a marriage-feast on Hampstead Heath.
Of course the people came in uncompelled,
Lame, blind, and worse — sick, sorrowful, and worse —
The humours of the peccant social wound
All pressed out, poured down upon Pimlico,
Exasperating the unaccustomed air
With a hideous interfusion.   You'd suppose
A finished generation, dead of plague,
Swept outward from their graves into the sun,
The moil of death upon them.   What a sight !   550
A holiday of miserable men
Is sadder than a burial-day of kings.
They clogged the streets, they oozed into the church
In a dark slow stream, like blood.   To see that sight,
The noble ladies stood up in their pews,
Some pale for fear, a few as red for hate,
Some simply curious, some just insolent,
And some in wondering scorn, — "What next ?
    what next ? "
These crushed their delicate rose-lips from the smile
That misbecame them in a holy place,   560
With broidered hems of perfumed handkerchiefs ;
Those passed the salts, with confidence of eyes
And simultaneous shiver of moiré silk :

While all the aisles, alive and black with heads,
Crawled slowly toward the altar from the street,
As bruised snakes crawl and hiss out of a hole
With shuddering involution, swaying slow
From right to left, and then from left to right,
In pants and pauses.   What an ugly crest
Of faces rose upon you everywhere   570
From that crammed mass ! you did not usually
See faces like them in the open day :
They hide in cellars, not to make you mad
As Romney Leigh is. — Faces ! — O my God,
We call those, faces ? men's and women's . . . ay,
And children's ; — babies, hanging like a rag
Forgotten on their mother's neck, — poor mouths,
Wiped clean of mother's milk by mother's blow
Before they are taught her cursing.   Faces ? . . .
      phew,
We'll call them vices, festering to despairs,   580
Or sorrows, petrifying to vices : not
A finger-touch of God left whole on them,
All ruined, lost — the countenance worn out
As the garment, the will dissolute as the act,
The passions loose and draggling in the dirt
To trip a foot up at the first free step !
Those, faces ? 'twas as if you had stirred up hell
To heave its lowest dreg-fiends uppermost
In fiery swirls of slime, — such strangled fronts,
Such obdurate jaws were thrown up constantly   590
To twit you with your race, corrupt your blood,
And grind to devilish colours all your dreams
Henceforth, — though, haply, you should drop asleep
By clink of silver waters, in a muse
On Raffael's mild Madonna of the Bird.

I've waked and slept through many nights and days
Since then, — but still that day will catch my breath
Like a nightmare.   There are fatal days, indeed,
In which the fibrous years have taken root
So deeply, that they quiver to their tops   600
Whene'er you stir the dust of such a day.

My cousin met me with his eyes and hand,
And then, with just a word, . . . that " Marian
        Erle
Was coming with her bridesmaids presently,"
Made haste to place me by the altar-stair
Where he and other noble gentlemen
And high-born ladies waited for the bride.

We waited.   It was early : there was time
For greeting and the morning's compliment,
And gradually a ripple of women's talk   610
Arose and fell and tossed about a spray
Of English _s_'s, soft as a silent hush,
And, notwithstanding, quite as audible
As louder phrases thrown out by the men.
— " Yes, really, if we need to wait in church,
We need to talk there." — " She ? 'tis Lady Ayr,
In blue — not purple ! that's the dowager."
— " She looks as young " — " She flirts as young,
        you mean.
Why, if you had seen her upon Thursday night, 619
You'd call Miss Norris modest." — " _You_ again !
I waltzed with you three hours back.   Up at six,
Up still at ten ; scarce time to change one's shoes :
I feel as white and sulky as a ghost,
So pray don't speak to me, Lord Belcher." — " No,
I'll look at you instead, and it's enough

While you have that face."   " In church, my lord !
 fie, fie ! ''
— " Adair, you stayed for the Division ? '' — " Lost
By one.''   " The devil it is !   I'm sorry for't.
And if I had not promised Mistress Grove ''   . . .
" You might have kept your word to Liverpool.'' 630
— " Constituents must remember, after all,
We're mortal.'' — " We remind them of it.'' —
 " Hark,
The bride comes ! here she comes, in a stream of
 milk ! ''
— '' There ?   Dear, you are asleep still ; don't you
 know
The five Miss Granvilles ? always dressed in white
To show they're ready to be married.'' — " Lower !
The aunt is at your elbow.'' — " Lady Maud,
Did Lady Waldemar tell you she had seen
This girl of Leigh's ? ''   " No, — wait ! 'twas
 Mistress Brookes,
Who told me Lady Waldemar told her —   640
No, 'twasn't Mistress Brookes.'' — " She's pretty ? ''
— " Who ?
Mistress Brookes ?   Lady Waldemar ? '' — " How
 hot !
Pray is't the law to-day we're not to breathe ?
You're treading on my shawl — I thank you, sir.''
— '' They say the bride's a mere child, who can't
 read,
But knows the things she shouldn't, with wide-awake
Great eyes.   I'd go through fire to look at her.''
— " You do, I think.'' — " And Lady Waldemar
(You see her ; sitting close to Romney Leigh.
How beautiful she looks, a little flushed !)   650
Has taken up the girl, and methodised

Leigh's folly.   Should I have come here, you suppose,
Except she'd asked me ?'' — ''She'd have served
      him more
By marrying him herself.''

                              '' Ah — there she comes,
The bride, at last ! ''

                              '' Indeed, no.   Past eleven.
She puts off her patched petticoat to-day
And puts on Mayfair manners, so begins
By setting us to wait.'' — '' Yes, yes, this Leigh
Was always odd ; it's in the blood, I think ;
His father's uncle's cousin's second son   660
Was, was . . . you understand me ; and for him,
He's stark, — has turned quite lunatic upon
This modern question of the poor — the poor.
An excellent subject when you're moderate ;
You've seen Prince Albert's model lodging-house ?
Does honour to his Royal Highness.   Good !
But would he stop his carriage in Cheapside
To shake a common fellow by the fist
Whose name was . . . Shakespeare ?   No.   We
      draw a line,
And if we stand not by our order, we   670
In England, we fall headlong.   Here's a sight, —
A hideous sight, a most indecent sight !
My wife would come, sir, or I had kept her back.
By heaven, sir, when poor Damiens' trunk and limbs
Were torn by horses, women of the court
Stood by and stared, exactly as to-day
On this dismembering of society,
With pretty, troubled faces.''

                              '' Now, at last.
She comes now.''

                              '' Where ? who sees ? you push me, sir,

Beyond the point of what is mannerly.   680
You're standing, madam, on my second flounce.
I do beseech you . . ."

"No — it's not the bride.
Half-past eleven. How late. The bridegroom, mark,
Gets anxious and goes out."

"And as I said,
These Leighs ! our best blood running in the rut !
It's something awful.   We had pardoned him
A simple misalliance got up aside
For a pair of sky-blue eyes ; the House of Lords
Has winked at such things, and we've all been young ;
But here's an intermarriage reasoned out,   690
A contract (carried boldly to the light
To challenge observation, pioneer
Good acts by a great example) 'twixt the extremes
Of martyrised society, — on the left
The well-born, on the right the merest mob,
To treat as equals ! — 'tis anarchical ;
It means more than it says ; 'tis damnable.
Why, sir, we can't have even our coffee good,
Unless we strain it."

"Here, Miss Leigh ! "

"Lord Howe,
You're Romney's friend.   What's all this waiting
    for ? "   700

" I cannot tell.   The bride has lost her head
(And way, perhaps !) to prove her sympathy
With the bridegroom."

" What, — you also, disapprove ! "

" Oh, *I* approve of nothing in the world,"
He answered, " not of you, still less of me,

Nor even of Romney, though he's worth us both.
We're all gone wrong.   The tune in us is lost ;
And whistling down back alleys to the moon
Will never catch it."

                                   Let me draw Lord Howe.
A born aristocrat, bred radical,   710
And educated socialist, who still
Goes floating, on traditions of his kind,
Across the theoretic flood from France,
Though, like a drenched Noah on a rotten deck,
Scarce safer for his place there.   He, at least,
Will never land on Ararat, he knows,
To recommence the world on the new plan :
Indeed, he thinks, said world had better end.
He sympathises rather with the fish   719
Outside, than with the drowned paired beasts within
Who cannot couple again or multiply, —
And that's the sort of Noah he is, Lord Howe.
He never could be anything complete,
Except a loyal, upright gentleman,
A liberal landlord, graceful diner-out,
And entertainer more than hospitable,
Whom authors dine with and forget the hock.
Whatever he believes, and it is much,
But nowise certain, now here and now there,
He still has sympathies beyond his creed   730
Diverting him from action.   In the House,
No party counts upon him, while for all
His speeches have a noticeable weight.
Men like his books too (he has written books),
Which, safe to lie beside a bishop's chair,
At times outreach themselves with jets of fire
At which the foremost of the progressists
May warm audacious hands in passing by.

Of stature over-tall, lounging for ease ;
Light hair, that seems to carry a wind in it,   740
And eyes that, when they look on you, will lean
Their whole weight, half in indolence and half
In wishing you unmitigated good,
Until you know not if to flinch from him
Or thank him. — 'Tis Lord Howe.

              "We're all gone wrong,"
Said he ; "and Romney, that dear friend of ours,
Is nowise right.   There's one true thing on earth,
That's love ! he takes it up, and dresses it,
And acts a play with it, as Hamlet did,
To show what cruel uncles we have been,   750
And how we should be uneasy in our minds
While he, Prince Hamlet, weds a pretty maid
(Who keeps us too long waiting, we'll confess)
By symbol, to instruct us formally
To fill the ditches up 'twixt class and class,
And live together in phalansteries.
What then ? — he's mad, our Hamlet ! clap his play,
And bind him."

        "Ah, Lord Howe, this spectacle
Pulls stronger at us than the Dane's.   See there !
The crammed aisles heave and strain and steam with
    life.   760
Dear Heaven, what life !"

        "Why, yes, — a poet sees ;
Which makes him different from a common man.
I, too, see somewhat, though I cannot sing ;
I should have been a poet, only that
My mother took fright at the ugly world,
And bore me tongue-tied.   If you'll grant me now
That Romney gives us a fine actor-piece
To make us merry on his marriage-morn,

The fable's worse than Hamlet's I'll concede.
The terrible people, old and poor and blind,   770
Their eyes eat out with plague and poverty
From seeing beautiful and cheerful sights,
We'll liken to a brutalised King Lear,
Led out,—by no means to clear scores with wrongs —
His wrongs are so far back, he has forgot
(All's past like youth); but just to witness here
A simple contract, — he, upon his side,
And Regan with her sister Goneril
And all the dappled courtiers and court-fools
On their side.   Not that any of these would say 780
They're sorry, neither.   What is done, is done,
And violence is now turned privilege,
As cream turns cheese, if buried long enough.
What could such lovely la'dies have to do
With the old man there, in those ill-odorous rags,
Except to keep the wind-side of him ?   Lear
Is flat and quiet, as a decent grave ;
He does not curse his daughters in the least :
Be these his daughters ?   Lear is thinking of
His porridge chiefly . . . is it getting cold   790
At Hampstead ? will the ale be served in pots ?
Poor Lear, poor daughters ! Bravo, Romney's play !''
A murmur and a movement drew around,
A naked whisper touched us.   Something wrong.
What's wrong ?   The black crowd, as an over-
        strained
Cord, quivered in vibration, and I saw . . .
Was that *his* face I saw ? . . . his . . . Romney
        Leigh's . . .
Which tossed a sudden horror like a sponge
Into all eyes, — while himself stood white upon
The topmost altar-stair and tried to speak,   800

And failed, and lifted higher above his head
A letter, . . . as a man who drowns and gasps.

"My brothers, bear with me! I am very weak.
I meant but only good. Perhaps I meant
Too proudly, and God snatched the circumstance
And changed it therefore. There's no marriage —
    none.
She leaves me, — she departs, — she disappears, —
I lose her. Yet I never forced her 'ay,'
To have her 'no' so cast into my teeth
In manner of an accusation, thus.   810
My friends, you are dismissed. Go, eat and drink
According to the programme, — and farewell!"
He ended. There was silence in the church.
We heard a baby sucking in its sleep
At the farthest end of the aisle. Then spoke a man:
"Now, look to it, coves, that all the beef and drink
Be not filched from us like the other fun,
For beer's spilt easier than a woman's lost!
This gentry is not honest with the poor;   819
They bring us up, to trick us." — "Go it, Jim,"
A woman screamed back, — "I'm a tender soul,
I never banged a child at two years old
And drew blood from him, but I sobbed for it
Next moment, — and I've had a plague of seven.
I'm tender; I've no stomach even for beef,
Until I know about the girl that's lost,
That's killed, mayhap. I did misdoubt, at first,
The fine lord meant no good by her or us.
He, maybe, got the upper hand of her
By holding up a wedding-ring, and then . . .   830
A choking finger on her throat last night,
And just a clever tale to keep us still,

As she is, poor lost innocent.   ' Disappear ! '
Who ever disappears except a ghost ?
And who believes a story of a ghost ?
I ask you, — would a girl go off, instead
Of staying to be married ? a fine tale !
A wicked man, I say, a wicked man !
For my part, I would rather starve on gin
Than make my dinner on his beef and beer.'' — 840
At which a cry rose up — '' We'll have our rights.
We'll have the girl, the girl !   Your ladies there
Are married safely and smoothly every day,
And *she* shall not drop through into a trap
Because she's poor and of the people : shame
We'll have no tricks played off by gentlefolk ;
We'll see her righted.''

                Through the rage and roar
I heard the broken words which Romney flung
Among the turbulent masses, from the ground
He held still with his masterful pale face, —   850
As huntsmen throw the ration to the pack,
Who, falling on it headlong, dog on dog
In heaps of fury, rend it, swallow it up
With yelling hound-jaws, — his indignant words,
His suppliant words, his most pathetic words,
Whereof I caught the meaning here and there
By his gesture . . . torn in morsels, yelled across,
And so devoured.   From end to end, the church
Rocked round us like the sea in storm, and then
Broke up like the earth in earthquake.   Men cried
       out   860
'' Police '' — and women stood and shrieked for God,
Or dropped and swooned ; or, like a herd of deer
(For whom the black woods suddenly grow alive,
Unleashing their wild shadows down the wind

To hunt the creatures into corners, back
And forward), madly fled, or blindly fell,
Trod screeching underneath the feet of those
Who fled and screeched.

              The last sight left to me
Was Romney's terrible calm face above   869
The tumult ! — the last sound was " Pull him down !
Strike — kill him ! " Stretching my unreasoning arms,
As men in dreams, who vainly interpose
'Twixt gods and their undoing, with a cry
I struggled to precipitate myself
Head-foremost to the rescue of my soul
In that white face, . . . till some one caught me
    back,
And so the world went out, — I felt no more.

What followed was told after by Lord Howe,
Who bore me senseless from the strangling crowd
In church and street, and then returned alone   880
To see the tumult quelled.   The men of law
Had fallen as thunder on a roaring fire,
And made all silent, — while the people's smoke
Passed eddying slowly from the emptied aisles.

Here's Marian's letter, which a ragged child
Brought running, just as Romney at the porch
Looked out expectant of the bride.   He sent
The letter to me by his friend Lord Howe
Some two hours after, folded in a sheet
On which his well-known hand had left a word. 890
Here's Marian's letter.

               " Noble friend, dear saint,
Be patient with me.   Never think me vile
Who might to-morrow morning be your wife

But that I loved you more than such a name.
Farewell, my Romney.   Let me write it once,—
My Romney.

    " 'Tis so pretty a coupled word,
I have no heart to pluck it with a blot.
We say 'my God' sometimes, upon our knees,
Who is not therefore vexed : so bear with it . . .
And me.   I know I'm foolish, weak, and vain : 900
Yet most of all I'm angry with myself
For losing your last footstep on the stair
That last time of your coming,— yesterday !
The very first time I lost step of yours
(Its sweetness comes the next to what you speak),
But yesterday sobs took me by the throat
And cut me off from music.

     " Mister Leigh,
You'll set me down as wrong in many things.
You've praised me, sir, for truth,— and now you'll learn
I had not courage to be rightly true.   910
I once began to tell you how she came,
The woman . . .   and you stared upon the floor
In one of your fixed thoughts . . .   which put me out
For that day.   After, some one spoke of me,
So wisely, and of you, so tenderly,
Persuading me to silence for your sake . . .
Well, well ! it seems this moment I was wrong
In keeping back from telling you the truth :
There might be truth betwixt us two, at least,
If nothing else.   And yet 'twas dangerous. 920
Suppose a real angel came from heaven
To live with men and women ! he'd go mad,
If no considerate hand should tie a blind

Across his piercing eyes.   'Tis thus with you :
You see us too much in your heavenly light ;
I always thought so, angel,— and indeed
There's danger that you beat yourself to death
Against the edges of this alien world,
In some divine and fluttering pity.

         " Yes,
It would be dreadful for a friend of yours,   930
To see all England thrust you out of doors
And mock you from the windows.   You might say,
Or think (that's worse) ' There's some one in the
    house
I miss and love still.'   Dreadful !

          " Very kind,
I pray you mark, was Lady Waldemar.
She came to see me nine times, rather ten —
So beautiful, she hurts one like the day
Let suddenly on sick eyes.

        " Most kind of all,
Your cousin ! — ah, most like you !   Ere you came
She kissed me mouth to mouth : I felt her soul   940
Dip through her serious lips in holy fire.
God help me, but it made me arrogant ;
I almost told her that you would not lose
By taking her to wife : though ever since
I've pondered much a certain thing she asked . . .
' He loves you, Marian ? ' . . . in a sort of mild
Derisive sadness . . . as a mother asks
Her babe, ' You'll touch that star, you think ? '

           " Farewell !
I know I never touched it.

        " This is worst :
Babes grow and lose the hope of things above ;   950
A silver threepence sets them leaping high —

But no more stars ! mark that.

                              " I've writ all night
Yet told you nothing.   God, if I could die,
And let this letter break off innocent
Just here !   But no — for your sake.

                              " Here's the last :
I never could be happy as your wife,
I never could be harmless as your friend,
I never will look more into your face
Till God says ' Look !' I charge you, seek me not,
Nor vex yourself with lamentable thoughts   960
That peradventure I have come to grief ;
Be sure I'm well, I'm merry, I'm at ease,
But such a long way, long way, long way off,
I think you'll find me sooner in my grave,
And that's my choice, observe.   For what remains,
An over generous friend will care for me
And keep me happy . . . happier . . .

                              " There's a blot !
This ink runs thick . . . we light girls lightly
      weep . . .
And keep me happier . . . was the thing to say,
Than as your wife I could be. — O, my star,   970
My saint, my soul ! for surely you're my soul,
Through whom God touched me ! I am not so lost
I cannot thank you for the good you did,
The tears you stopped, which fell down bitterly,
Like these — the times you made me weep for joy
At hoping I should learn to write your notes
And save the tiring of your eyes, at night ;
And most for that sweet thrice you kissed my lips
Saying ' Dear Marian.'

                              " 'Twould be hard to read,
This letter, for a reader half as learn'd ;   980

But you'll be sure to master it in spite
Of ups and downs.   My hand shakes, I am blind ;
I'm poor at writing at the best,— and yet
I tried to make my *g*'s the way you showed.
Farewell.   Christ love you.— Say ' poor **Marian**'
    now."
Poor Marian !— wanton Marian !— was it so,
Or so ?   For days, her touching, foolish lines
We mused on with conjectural fantasy,
As if some riddle of a summer-cloud
On which one tries unlike similitudes   990
Of now a spotted Hydra-skin cast off,
And now a screen of carven ivory
That shuts the heavens' conventual secrets up
From mortals overbold.   We sought the sense :
She loved him so perhaps (such words mean love),
That, worked on by some shrewd perfidious tongue
(And then I thought of Lady Waldemar),
She left him, not to hurt him ; or perhaps
She loved one in her class,— or did not love,
But mused upon her wild bad tramping life   1000
Until the free blood fluttered at her heart,
And black bread eaten by the roadside hedge
Seemed sweeter than being put to Romney's school
Of philanthropical self-sacrifice
Irrevocably.— Girls are girls, beside,
Thought I, and like a wedding by one rule.
You seldom catch these birds except with chaff :
They feel it almost an immoral thing
To go out and be married in broad day,
Unless some winning special flattery should   1010
Excuse them to themselves for't, . . . " No one
    parts
Her hair with such a silver line as you,

One moonbeam from the forehead to the crown !''
Or else . . . " You bite your lip in such a way
It spoils me for the smiling of the rest,''
And so on.   Then a worthless gaud or two
To keep for love,— a ribbon for the neck,
Or some glass pin,— they have their weight with
     girls.
And Romney sought her many days and weeks :
He sifted all the refuse of the town,   1020
Explored the trains, inquired among the ships,
And felt the country through from end to end ;
No Marian ! — though I hinted what I knew,—
A friend of his had reasons of her own
For throwing back the match — he would not hear :
The lady had been ailing ever since,
The shock had harmed her.   Something in his tone
Repressed me ; something in me shamed my doubt
To a sigh repressed too.   He went on to say
That putting questions where his Marian lodged, 1030
He found she had received for visitors,
Besides himself and Lady Waldemar
And, that once, me — a dubious woman dressed
Beyond us both : the rings upon her hands
Had dazed the children when she threw them pence ;
" She wore her bonnet as the queen might hers,
To show the crown,'' they said, — " a scarlet crown
Of roses that had never been in bud.''

When Romney told me that, — for now and then
He came to tell me how the search advanced,   1040
His voice dropped : I bent forward for the rest :
The woman had been with her, it appeared,
At first from week to week, then day by day,
And last, 'twas sure . . .

                I looked upon the ground
To escape the anguish of his eyes, and asked
As low as when you speak to mourners new
Of those they cannot bear yet to call dead,
"If Marian had as much as named to him
A certain Rose, an early friend of hers,
A ruined creature."

                "Never." — Starting up   1050
He strode from side to side about the room,
Most like some prisoned lion sprung awake,
Who has felt the desert sting him through his dreams.
"What was I to her, that she should tell me aught ?
A friend ! was *I* a friend ?   I see all clear.
Such devils would pull angels out of heaven,
Provided they could reach them ; 'tis their pride ;
And that's the odds 'twixt soul and body plague !
The veriest slave who drops in Cairo's street
Cries ' Stand off from me ' to the passengers ;   1060
While these blotched souls are eager to infect,
And blow their bad breath in a sister's face
As if they got some ease by it."

                    I broke through.
"Some natures catch no plagues.   I've read of babes
Found whole and sleeping by the spotted breast
Of one a full day dead.   I hold it true,
As I'm a woman and know womanhood,
That Marian Erle, however lured from place,
Deceived in way, keeps pure in aim and heart
As snow that's drifted from the garden-bank   1070
To the open road."

             'Twas hard to hear him laugh.
"The figure's happy.   Well — a dozen carts
And trampers will secure you presently
A fine white snow-drift.   Leave it there, your snow :

'Twill pass for soot ere sunset.   Pure in aim ?
She's pure in aim, I grant you, — like myself,
Who thought to take the world upon my back
To carry it o'er a chasm of social ill,
And end by letting slip through impotence
A single soul, a child's weight in a soul,   1080
Straight down the pit of hell ! yes, I and she
Have reason to be proud of our pure aims."
Then softly, as the last repenting drops
Of a thunder-shower, he added, "The poor child,
Poor Marian ! 'twas a luckless day for her
When first she chanced on my philanthropy."

He drew a chair beside me, and sat down ;
And I, instinctively, as women use
Before a sweet friend's grief, — when, in his ear,
They hum the tune of comfort though themselves
Most ignorant of the special words of such,   1091
And quiet so and fortify his brain
And give it time and strength for feeling out
To reach the availing sense beyond that sound, —
Went murmuring to him what, if written here,
Would seem not much, yet fetched him better help
Than peradventure if it had been more.

I've known the pregnant thinkers of our time,
And stood by breathless, hanging on their lips,
When some chromatic sequence of fine thought   1100
In learned modulation phrased itself
To an unconjectured harmony of truth :
And yet I've been more moved, more raised, I say,
By a simple word . . . a broken easy thing
A three-years' infant might at need repeat,
A look, a sigh, a touch upon the palm,

Which meant less than " I love you," than by all
The full-voiced rhetoric of those master-mouths.

" Ah, dear Aurora," he began at last,
His pale lips fumbling for a sort of smile,   1110
" Your printer's devils have not spoilt your heart :
That's well.   And who knows but, long years ago
When you and I talked, you were somewhat right
In being so peevish with me ?   You, at least,
Have ruined no one through your dreams.   Instead,
You've helped the facile youth to live youth's day
With innocent distraction, still perhaps
Suggestive of things better than your rhymes.
The little shepherd-maiden, eight years old,
I've seen upon the mountains of Vaucluse,   1120
Asleep i' the sun, her head upon her knees,
The flocks all scattered, — is more laudable
Than any sheep-dog, trained imperfectly,
Who bites the kids through too much zeal."

                                        " I look

As if I had slept, then ! "

                              He was touched at once
By something in my face.   Indeed 'twas sure
That he and I, — despite a year or two
Of younger life on my side, and on his
The heaping of the years' work on the days,
The three-hour speeches from the member's seat,   1130
The hot committees in and out of doors,
The pamphlets, " Arguments," " Collective Views,"
Tossed out as straw before sick houses, just
To show one's sick and so be trod to dirt
And no more use, — through this world's under-
          ground,
The burrowing, groping effort, whence the arm

And heart come torn, — 'twas sure that he and I
Were, after all, unequally fatigued ;
That he, in his developed manhood, stood
A little sunburnt by the glare of life,   1140
While I . . . it seemed no sun had shone on me,
So many seasons I had missed my Springs.
My cheeks had pined and perished from their orbs,
And all the youth-blood in them had grown white
As dew on autumn cyclamens : alone
My eyes and forehead answered for my face.

He said, " Aurora, you are changed — are ill ! "

" Not so, my cousin, — only not asleep,"
I answered, smiling gently.   " Let it be.
You scarcely found the poet of Vaucluse   1150
As drowsy as the shepherds.   What is art
But life upon the larger scale, the higher,
When, graduating up in a spiral line
Of still expanding and ascending gyres,
It pushes toward the intense significance
Of all things, hungry for the Infinite ?
Art's life, — and where we live, we suffer and toil."

He seemed to sift me with his painful eyes.
" You take it gravely, cousin ; you refuse   1159
Your dreamland's right of common, and green rest.
You break the mythic turf where danced the nymphs,
With crooked ploughs of actual life, — let in
The axes to the legendary woods,
To pay the poll-tax.   You are fallen indeed
On evil days, you poets, if yourselves
Can praise that art of yours no otherwise ;
And, if you cannot, . . . better take a trade
And be of use : 'twere cheaper for your youth."

" Of use ! " I softly echoed, " there's the point
We sweep about for ever in argument,   1170
Like swallows which the exasperate, dying year
Sets spinning in black circles, round and round,
Preparing for far flights o'er unknown seas.
And we, where tend we ? "

                " Where ? " he said, and sighed.
" The whole creation, from the hour we are born,
Perplexes us with questions.   Not a stone
But cries behind us, every weary step,
' Where, where ? '   I leave stones to reply to stones.
Enough for me and for my fleshy heart
To hearken the invocations of my kind,   1180
When men catch hold upon my shuddering nerves
And shriek ' What help ? what hope ? what bread i'
    the house,
' What fire i' the frost ? '   There must be some
    response,
Though mine fail utterly.   This social Sphinx
Who sits between the sepulchres and stews,
Makes mock and mow against the crystal heavens,
And bullies God, — exacts a word at least
From each man standing on the side of God,
However paying a sphinx-price for it.
We pay it also if we hold our peace,   1190
In pangs and pity.   Let me speak and die.
Alas, you'll say I speak and kill instead."
I pressed in there.   " The best men, doing their best,
Know peradventure least of what they do :
Men usefullest i' the world are simply used ;
The nail that holds the wood must pierce it first,
And He alone who wields the hammer sees
The work advanced by the earliest blow.   Take
    heart."

"Ah, if I could have taken yours ! " he said,
"But that's past now."   Then rising, — "I will
    take   1200
At least your kindness and encouragement.
I thank you.   Dear, be happy.   Sing your songs,
If that's your way ! but sometimes slumber too,
Nor tire too much with following, out of breath,
The rhymes upon your mountains of Delight.
Reflect, if Art be in truth the higher life,
You need the lower life to stand upon
In order to reach up unto that higher ;
And none can stand a-tip toe in the place
He cannot stand in with two stable feet.   1210
Remember then ! — for Art's sake, hold your life."

We parted so.   I held him in respect.
I comprehended what he was in heart
And sacrificial greatness.   Ay, but he
Supposed me a thing too small, to deign to know :
He blew me, plainly, from the crucible
As some intruding, interrupting fly,
Not worth the pains of his analysis
Absorbed on nobler subjects.   Hurt a fly !
He would not for the world : he's pitiful   1220
To flies even.   "Sing, " says he, "and tease me
    still,
If that's your way, poor insect."   That's your way !

NOTES.

AURORA LEIGH.

A POEM IN NINE BOOKS. 1856.

Aurora Leigh. First Book. Aurora, still very young, recalls some childish memories of her mother and then tells the story of her early life — how her father, an austere Englishman, had gone to Florence for a month for the purpose of studying the secret of some of Da Vinci's engineering works, and while there saw in a church procession a beautiful young Florentine girl, with whom he immediately fell in love. He married her, but a few years later she died, leaving the little Aurora, four years old. The father then left Florence and retired to the mountains in the country, for he believed that his child, deprived of her mother as she was, needed the more the influence of Mother Nature. There they lived for nine years, the child's imagination centred upon her mother's portrait, which became in her eyes now one, now another creature of fancy grown familiar to her in her studies and reading, while her father taught her "what he knew best, love and grief," and as she says later, all he knew of Latin and Greek, regardless of its fitness for a child.

When she was thirteen her father died, and the grief-stricken child was sent to England to live with her maiden aunt, a well-meaning but unsympathetic person who had never forgiven her brother for marrying an Italian.

She gives an account of the studies her aunt thought it fitting for her to pursue, which include religious doctrines, history, geography, music, painting, embroidery, and so on, a system of education which, though its shallowness met with Aurora's scorn, was endured by her.

She, however, began to pine under this *régime* and looked so pale that her aunt's neighbors said she would certainly die.   In this unsympathetic atmosphere her cousin Romney was something of a friend, though their natures differed : she was an idealist, looking always for the gods, while the woes of humanity weighed heavily upon his mind.

Though she was not inclined to respond to the interest her cousin Romney took in her, she began to revive, partly through his kindness, she thinks.   The beauty of the world about her had its effect upon her, too, and she found herself beginning to enjoy reading her own books in her own little room, thinking her own thoughts, and then slipping out to wander on the hills before the others were up in the morning.   Her reading included books good and bad, and in spite of the dangers to a young mind in having evil presented in the guise of beauty as it often appears in the book-world, she breasted her way through all these deeps of knowledge and found herself ever brought nearer to the central truth.   All these books she discovered in a garret, in boxes with her father's name, and in fear and trembling stole off with them, putting a book under her pillow at night and anxiously waiting for the sun to rise so that she might begin to read it.

Thus it was she chanced upon the poets, who opened a new world to her.

From here to the end of the book she talks about the poets and her own aspirations toward poetry, claiming for poets the rôle of "the only speakers of essential truth."   Doubtful of her own powers, she is yet intoxicated with the idea of becoming a poet, and begins to write poems which she describes as having the false note of imitation and pretended agedness frequently characteristic of youthful poems.

Her aunt, noticing the "soul agaze" in her eyes, and being afraid of souls, keeps her all the more closely to her tasks, but the new inner life brings fresh vigor to Aurora, and happy in her newfound power she resolves to live, and in thus living a true life learns to love her father's land, and to enjoy her rambles alone or with Romney and his friend the painter, Vincent Carrington, and thus ends the first stage of her development.

Lines 10–14. *I have not so far left the coasts of life, etc.* : compare with the closing of the ninth stanza of Wordsworth's "Ode on the Intimations of Immortality."

24. *Scudi:* plural of scudo. Formerly a Roman gold coin worth about $15.70. Now the name of an Italian coin worth about $1.02.

57. *Love's Divine Which burns and hurts not:* a reference to the bush in Exodus iii., 2 — "And the angel of the Lord appeared unto him in a flame of fire out of the midst of a bush : and he looked, and, behold, the bush burned with fire, and the bush was not consumed."

72. *Da Vinci's drains:* this great artist (1452–1519) was also distinguished as an architect and engineer, and among other things constructed the aqueduct which supplies Milan with water.

77. *Square of the Santissima:* in front of the fine church Santissima Annunziata, founded in 1250.

80–85. *A train of priestly banners, etc.:* this is a description of a church festival such as they still have in Italy in honor of the saints or of certain events in the life of Jesus or Mary, or Joseph, etc. This might have been a festival in honor of the Purification of the Blessed Virgin, or as it is popularly called, the Festival of Candles, because the tapers which the faithful carry in procession to the church are blessed.

102. *Santa Croce:* this church dates back to 1297, when it was begun by Franciscan monks, though little remains of the original building. It is striking from its size and is almost surrounded by monuments of great men.

Line 111. *The mountains above Pelago:* a picturesque village not far from Florence. From it a steep path through pine woods ascends to upland meadows covered with flowers and watered by running streams, and not far off is the convent of Vallombrosa, surrounded by more woods and mountains.

114. *And Pan's white goats:* goats were sacred to Pan, the god with the goat thighs and hoofs and horns. After her manner the poet makes her own variation on the myth and symbolizes the stimulus to be derived from nature as the milk of the white goats of Pan, the nature god.

130. *Cameriera:* waiting woman or maid.

132. *Pitti:* this magnificent palace is almost opposite to Casa Guidi, where Mrs. Browning wrote most of "Aurora Leigh." Hare says that it was begun in 1441 from a design of Brunelleschi (though this is doubted by some) by Luca Pitti, and was sold by his descendants in 1549 to the first Eleanora of Toledo, wife of Cosimo I. It was long the residence of the grand-dukes, and is now occupied by King Victor Emmanuel.

156. *A loving Psyche who loses sight of Love:* a reference to the incident in the myth of Psyche and Cupid where, her curiosity getting the better of her because she has been told her husband is a monster, she takes a lamp and gazes on the sleeping Cupid. A drop of oil from the lamp falling upon Cupid awakes him, and he flies off, leaving her forever, because love cannot live with suspicion. (See Gayley's "Classic Myths in English Literature" for an account of the story, which is told by Apuleius, 2d Century, in his Metamorphoses or "The Golden Ass." Also Mrs. Browning's translations from Apuleius in Vol. VI., this edition.)

157. *Medusa:* the most celebrated of the three gorgons, Stheno, Euryale, and Medusa, children of Pontus and Ceto, whose glance was icy death.

The gorgon Medusa was a terrible being, against whom Perseus went in order to free the country from her

ravages.   At one time she had been a maiden whose hair
was her chief glory, but she had the audacity to vie with
Minerva, whereupon that goddess deprived her of her
charms and changed her beautiful curls into hissing
serpents.   After this she turned into stone whoever beheld
her.   Perseus found her in the hall of the gorgons along
with her two silent sisters, and either as she moaned and
prayed that her misery might be ended, or as she slept,
Perseus, guided by her image reflected in his shield, cut off
her head.   (See Ovid, Metamorphoses, iv., 608–739 ; v.,
1–249.)

Line 160.   *Our Lady of the Passion, stabbed with swords :*
the Virgin Mary is sometimes represented in pictures and
in religious processions in Italy stabbed with swords,
which are symbolical of the seven sorrows of " Our
Lady."   (Compare with Robert Browning's " Up at a
Villa Down in the City," lines 51–52, Vol. iv., *Camberwell Browning.*)

161.   *Lamia in her first Moonlighted pallor, etc.* : there
was an ancient superstition to the effect that a monster
with a face and upper part like the body of a woman,
and extremities like a serpent, used to inhabit Africa.   In
Greek myth there was a Lamia, daughter of Belus, who,
on account of Jupiter's love for her, was changed by
Juno into a monster, said to feed on man's flesh.   According to another account, becoming insane because of
Juno's jealousy, she caught and devoured all new-
born children.   The Lamias of the ancients were also
sometimes represented as a kind of monstrous animal.
The reference here, however, is to the poem " Lamia "
by Keats, which he developed from a passage he found
in Burton's " Anatomy of Melancholy " as follows :

" Philostratus, in his fourth book *de Vita Apollonii,*
hath a memorable instance in kind, which I may not
omit, of one Menippus Lycius, a young man twenty-five
years of age that, going betwixt Cenchreas and Corinth,
met such a phantasm in the habit of a fair gentlewoman,
which, taking him by the hand, carried him home to her

house, in the suburbs of Corinth, and told him she was
a Phœnician by birth, and if he would tarry with her, he
should hear her sing and play, and drink such wine as
never any drank, and no man should molest him ; but
she, being fair and lovely, would die with him that was
fair and lovely to behold.   The young man, a philosopher, otherwise staid and discreet, able to moderate his
passions, though not this of love, tarried with her awhile
to his great content, and at last married her, to whose
wedding, amongst other guests, came Apollonius ; who,
by some probable conjectures, found her out to be a serpent, a lamia ; and that all her furniture was, like Tan-
talus' gold, described by Homer, no substance, but mere
illusions.   When she saw herself descried, she wept, and
desired Apollonius to be silent, but he would not be
moved, and thereupon she, plate, house, and all that was
in it, vanished in an instant ; many thousands took notice
of this fact, for it was done in the midst of Greece.''

The passages in Keats's poem illustrating Mrs. Browning's reference are as follows :

> "' Begone, foul dream ! ' he cried gazing again
> In the bride's face, where now no azure vein
> Wander'd on fair-spaced temples ; no soft bloom
> Misted the cheek ; no passion to illume
> The deep-recessed vision : — all was blight ;
> Lamia, no longer fair, there sat a deadly white.
>
> .   .   .   .
>
>   She, as well
> As her weak hand could any meaning tell,
> Motion'd him to be silent ; vainly so,
> He look'd and look'd again a level — No !
> ' A serpent ! ' echoed he ; no sooner said,
> Than with a frightful scream she vanished."

Lines 176–184.   *My father   .   .   .   broken loose From
chinbands of the soul, like Lazarus, etc.*: the idea expressed
in this passage, that Lazarus, after having been raised from
the dead, lost his actual grip upon life, and his sense of

tne relations of things, through having gained a glimpse
from God's point of view, is fully developed in Robert
Browning's " An Epistle : containing the Strange Medical Experience of Karshish the Arab Physician.''   This
poem appeared the year before '' Aurora Leigh,'' in
1855, but as Mrs. Browning had been engaged upon
" Aurora Leigh '' since 1852, the idea was probably
original with her.

Line 221. *That it should eat and end itself Like some
tormented scorpion :* this formidable insect resembles a
spider, but its front legs are developed into large claws
that look like a lobster's, while it has a tail which emits
from two small orifices at the end a poisonous fluid.
The fact that scorpions sometimes commit suicide was
long thought to be only a popular fable, but recently actual proof has been forthcoming from eye-witnesses that
a scorpion subjected to heat or sudden light will rush
about in an excited manner for some time, and then
plunge its own sting into its head.

251. *The frosty cliffs Looked cold upon me :* the white
chalk cliffs at Dover, which have a snow-like effect as the
coast is approached.

265. *God's celestial crystals :* a reminiscence perhaps
of the ancient notion that the sky was a crystalline
sphere beyond the stars, which moved around the central
earth as the sun, moon, and stars did.

390. *Bene :* it is well. — *Che che :* no, indeed.

392 *The collects :* parts of the ritual of the English
Episcopal Church, to be found in any English prayer-
book. — *Catechism* : questions meant for the religious
instruction of the young, and considered very important
in the Church of England.

393. *The creeds, from Athanasius back to Nice :* the
Athanasian creed was supposed to have been drawn up
by Athanasius in the fourth century. There is not, however, sufficient proof of this, authorities differing as to
whom it should be attributed to. It is known especially
for its damnatory clauses and is now generally discarded on

that account. The Nicene Creed was drawn up at the council of Nice, A.D. 325, with a view to combating certain heresies, especially those of Arianism.

Line 394. *The Articles:* the thirty-nine articles contain the confession of faith of the Church of England as it was evolved from 1549, when Cranmer drew up a series of articles, to 1571, when the clergy in convocation adopted them as they now stand. — *Tracts against the Times:* allusion to the "Tracts for the Times," written mostly by Newman, Pusey, and Keble, against the party of Church reform. The popular voice called for an adaptation of the church to the spirit of the age, and the Tractarians took reactionary measures, defended the rights of the clergy, the principle of salvation through the sacraments, and the exclusive authority of the visible church. The poet implies her own standpoint by calling them Tracts *against* the times.

395. *Buonaventure's "Prick of Love"*: Saint Buonaventure (1221–1274), Cardinal and Bishop of Albano, was a celebrated writer on theology and philosophy, who followed the Platonizing and mystical mode of speculation. According to him, the intellect is of inferior interest when compared with the power of the heart. Reason can discover some of the moral truths which form the groundwork of the Christian system, but others it can only receive through divine illumination. The soul may even rise to ecstatic union with God, and the supreme end of life is such union in intense, absorbing love. (See article "Bonaventura" in Encyclopædia Britannica.) The poet evidently refers here to the cardinal doctrine of his philosophy, namely, love, and she may have had in mind his book, *Itinerarium mentis ad meum*," the way of the soul to God. On account of his character he was called The Seraphic Doctor, and was canonized in 1482 by Sextus IV.

400. *Kept pure of Balzac and neologism:* Balzac (1799–1858), celebrated French writer of novels dealing with so much that is evil in life that they are not consid-

ered good reading for immature minds. He called himself "The Secretary of Society" who "drew up the
inventory of its vices and virtues." Neologism would be
equally bad for the young mind, for it was the precursor
of Rationalism. Without denying the value of the
Scriptures, it took the ground that they had frequently
been misunderstood, and explained the miracles according to natural powers and means. The word was first
used in Germany in the middle of the eighteenth century.

Line 407. *Royal genealogies Of Oviedo* : Oviedo (1478–
about 1558) was a Spanish historian who accompanied
Columbus on his first voyage to Hispaniola. He wrote
"A General History of the Indies," and also a book in
dialogue relating to the Genealogies and Revenues of the
Grandees of Spain. Evidently this is the book Mrs.
Browning is thinking of, though it is said never to have
been published.

409. *Burmese empire* : occupies an extensive tract in
India beyond the Ganges. Absolute despotism is the
form of government. The whole nation is divided into
the royal families, nobles, and commonalty. They have
no further system of caste, like that of the Hindus, but a
kind of feudalism prevails.

410. *Mount Chimborazo outsoars Teneriffe* : the first is
one of the highest peaks of the Andes in South America,
and is 21,424 feet above the sea ; the second is in the
Canary Islands, and is 11,400 feet above the sea.

412. *Lara* : there is a town in Spain of this name on
the river Arlanza.

413. *Klagenfurt* : a town and circle in Carinthia in
Austria. The population is made up of German and
Wends. A census taken in 1837 gave it at 178,523.
Perhaps Mrs. Browning had this census in mind, for, although an old town, it is doubtful if one was taken in the
year 5. There is a vein of humorous exaggeration running through this whole passage on her education.

416. *As quite impossible in Johnson's day* : an allusion
to the well-known story told of Dr. Johnson who, when

it was pointed out to him how difficult was a piece of
music a young lady was playing, replied, "Would that it
had been impossible."

Line 420.   *Tophet* : see Isaiah xxx., 33.

421.   *Nereids* : water nymphs that presided over rivers
and fountains.

424.   *Cellarius* : a kind of waltz.

454.   *The tortoise-shell Which slew the tragic poet* :
Æschylus, who according to the tradition was killed
while he was sitting meditating in a field, by an eagle,
which, mistaking his bald head for a stone, dropped a
tortoise on it to break the shell.

467.   *Brinvilliers suffered more In the water-torture* : Marie Marguerite, Marquise de Brinvilliers, a
celebrated criminal who was beheaded in 1676 for
poisoning, in order to secure their fortunes, the father,
brothers, and sister of her husband, for the sake of a
young man, St. Croix, with whom she was in love.
Madame de Sévigné writes that she entered the room
where the questioning is done, and seeing three buckets of
water, said, "It is assuredly to drown me, for from the
size that I am, they cannot intend me to drink all that."
The water torture consists in forcing water down the
throat.

536.   *The figs grow black as if by a Tuscan rock* : the
fig originally from the tropics has been cultivated in the
southern countries of Europe and America, and under
very favorable circumstances they will ripen or "grow
black " in England.

612.   *Alas, my Giotto's background* : in the early
Italian art the gold backgrounds, distinctive of Byzantine art, were frequently seen.   Aurora's thoughts here
fly from the golden sky to Giotto's golden backgrounds.
Giotto (1276–1336) exercised a lasting influence upon
art, he being the first to free himself from the stiffness of
the Byzantine models.

616.   *Vallombrosa* : convent or monastery beautifully
situated on high meadows just above the village of Pelago,

not far from Florence and surrounded by woods made
famous by Milton's allusion to them :

> " Thick as autumnal leaves that strew the brooks
> In Vallombrosa, where the Etrurian shades
> High over-arch'd imbower."
>
> ("Paradise Lost," i., 302.)

Line 674. *Apocalyptic :* from the Greek word meaning
" revelation,'' and applied to that especial kind of
prophecy through revelation that makes use of symbolical language as in the Apocalypse of John.

687. *At foolish unaware :* this is similar to the use of
" at unawares '' as an adverbial expression meaning unex-
pectedly, found in Dryden and others.

712. *Theophrast :* a Greek philosopher who was first
a disciple of Plato's, then of Aristotle's ; Aristotle admired him so much that he gave him the name Theo-
phrastus, " One who speaks divinely.'' Among his
books are " A Treatise on Plants,'' " A History of
Stones,'' and " Moral Characters.'' He was born about
370 B.C., and lived to be very old.

714. *Ælian :* an Italian historian and rhetorician who
wrote Greek, and lived either in the time of Adrian or of
Alexander Severus.

716. *Fives :* a kind of ball game that resembles ten-
nis, in which three fives count as the game.

723. *As did the women formerly By young Achilles, etc. :*
a reference to the story that in order to prevent Achilles
from going to the Trojan war, his mother, Thetis, knowing he would perish in the war, sent him to the court of
Lycomedes, king of the island of Scyros, where by his
mother's persuasion he disguised himself as a maiden,
and associated with the king's daughters, so concealing
his identity.

738. *Flies back to cover all that past with leaves :*
allusion to the well-known folk story of the two little
children who were lost in the woods, and died there and
were tenderly covered up with leaves by robins.

Line 756. *Saint Michael :* in Daniel this name is given to
one of the chief princes of the heavenly host, the guardian
angel of Israel.   He appears in Jewish theology as the
greatest of the angels, the first of the four who surround
the throne of God.   He is reverenced as a saint in the
Catholic church ; there is a special festival to Saint
Michael and all the angels.

766.   *Who distinguishes 'Twixt Saul and Nahash justly
at first sight :* see I. Samuel xi.

768.   *Leaves King Saul precisely at the sin, To serve
King David:* see the history of Saul and David in I.
Samuel, also II. Samuel iii.

771.   *For Alaric as well as Charlemagne*: Alaric
(about 400) as king of the Visigoths stands in the poet's
mind here for barbarism, while Charlemagne, who in 800
was crowned Emperor of the West by Pope Leo III.,
as a promoter of learning and a wise ruler, stands for
civilization.   Yet, as the whole passage suggests, who
can judge at first sight which contributes the most valuable elements of truth ?   Certainly not a child, and, by
implication, not even the wise.

815.   *Cygnet :* a young swan.

826.   *Palimpsest:* a parchment in which the original
writing has been erased either with pumice stone or
chemicals, and other writing put in its place.— *Holograph* :
an autograph manuscript.

827.   *Defiled, erased and covered by a monk's :* many
of the monkish manuscripts are palimpsests, valuable
ancient manuscripts having been destroyed in this way to
make room for some valueless disquisition on the saints.

828.   *The apocalypse, by a Longus :* a facetious remark
on the part of the poet, for Longus was a Greek writer
of romances, among which are " The Loves of Daphnis
and Chloe.''   He lived either in the fourth or fifth century.

831.   *Alpha and omega :* the first and last letters of the
Greek alphabet.

919-925.   *My eagle, with both grappling feet still hot*

From Zeus's thunder, etc. : in this passage Aurora applies to herself the story of Ganymede, who was carried off by Zeus in the form of an eagle (the bird sacred to Zeus) to become cup-bearer to the gods in Olympus.

Line 925.   *Everlasting   laughters :*   inextinguishable laughter of the gods is a phrase used by Homer, of which this is an echo, used to symbolize poetical inspiration.

929.   *We drop the golden cup at Heré's foot :* Heré, the wife of Zeus and queen of the gods, is here used to symbolize the climax of poetical power so dazzling that the poor cup-bearers faint and find themselves again upon the earth among the "sheep and cows" of every-day life. The whole passage is a splendid simile of the exaltation of the awakened artist soul.

938.   *Imposthumes :* abscesses, or as here used, humors.

941.   *Ape a Bourbon in a crown of straws :* the poet may have had especially in mind Louis XVII., son of Louis XVI. and Marie Antoinette, who was proclaimed king after his father's execution and recognized as such by England and Russia, but who died in captivity in the Temple, Paris, June 8, 1795 ; or, perhaps, Louis Philippe, who held his crown not by divine right but by the will of the people, as king of the French ; or she may have been thinking of the Bourbons as a whole during the revolutionary and Napoleonic *régime.*

964.   *Term :* or Terminus, the Roman god who presided over boundaries.

976.   *Touch not, do not taste, etc.* : see Colossians ii., 21.

978.   *Phorminx :* the name of the ancient Greek lyre, which had probably seven strings.

979.   *Counterpoint :* a musical device in which two or more melodies or parts are made to harmonize together ; here used to signify musical art in general.

985.   *Bucolics :* from the Greek word *bucolikas,* cow, poems describing rural affairs and the lives of shepherds.

990.   *Counterfeiting epics :* the poet was probably thinking of her own youthful epic, "The Battle of Marathon."

Line 1002. *Spare the old bottles!— spill not the new wine:*
that is, the fresh genius should be kept for better things
than the imitation of old forms which cannot fully express its thoughts. (For the allusion see Matthew ix., 17.)

1003–1014. *By Keats's soul, etc.:* in this passage the
poet points out a notable distinction between Keats, the
poet, who died at twenty years of age, leaving a body of
poetry of high artistic and emotional value, and Pope and
Byron, who were didactic and intellectual at this age.   It
might be questioned, however, whether Keats is the only
"excepted soul" proving the rule that young poets
write old, which simply means, as she suggests in the following lines, that they are imitative, or mix up memory
with vision.   Chaucer, Shakespeare, Spenser, Milton,
Coleridge, Wordsworth, and Shelley might all be mentioned as poets who early struck an individual note.   The
fact is emphasized, however, in the case of Keats, because of his very early death.

1020. *Muse-Sphinx:* the Muse of wisdom is perhaps
only to be discovered by viewing the past as well as aspiring toward the future.

1034. *Souls were dangerous things to carry straight
through all the spilt saltpetre of the world:* that is, the
soul is like a spark that might set fire to the gunpowder
(saltpetre is the chief ingredient in gunpowder) of dangerous enthusiasms latent in society.

1096. *Men judge hardly as bee-bonneted:* the expression, "he has a bee in his bonnet," is used of any one
who is hipped upon any subject.

1097. *Because he holds that, paint a body well, You paint
a soul by implication:* compare with Robert Browning's
"Fra Lippo Lippi," lines 199–201 :

> "Now is this sense, I ask?
> A fine way to paint soul, by painting body
> So ill, the eye can't stop there, must go further
> And can't fare worse."

(See *Camberwell Browning*, Vol. v.)

Second Book. In this book Aurora recalls the events of her twentieth birthday, and those which immediately followed. She trips out on her bright June birthday morning to enjoy a little personal freedom with nature before her aunt awakes and casts her chains around her.

Imagining herself a poet, in a spirit of sport she crowns herself with a wreath of ivy, and is confronted in the act by her cousin Romney. He has found a mislaid book in which she had written some poems, and takes advantage of this fact in returning it to express his disapproval of women's attempts to do anything in art, and in the usual manly way goes on to settle just what women's natures are like, and just what their sphere is. Their attitude toward life is narrow and personal, their sympathy aroused only by a direct appeal, hence they are incapable of taking a broad view of the general woe of the world. As they cannot comprehend the world, therefore the world cannot be influenced by them. Being personal and passionate, they succeed only in the rôle of wife and mother.

He then appeals to Aurora on the ground that she is too fine a woman to play at art.

Aurora breaks in here and assures him she quite agrees with him that a sublime art should not be pursued frivolously.

Upon this he begs her to choose nobler work and launches out into a description of the ills the poor are suffering from in these days when there is naught but the rich man and Lazarus with an impassable gulf between, and how he feels that he being a man must seek some cure for all these ills. To Aurora's question as to whether the world is really so bad, he assures her it is so bad that he cannot choose but vow away his years, means, and aims among the helpers.

She replies to this with a touch of sarcasm, lost upon Romney, that though she is incapable of comprehending these knotty social problems, that even a child may say

" Amen " to a bishop's prayer, and therefore she can approve his aims and give him her reverence.

He catches at this and asks if she can give him no other help, to which she very properly retorts that he would scorn any help a woman could give.

He then asks for what he declares a woman only can give, love and fellowship through bitter duties.

His wooing, however, does not please Aurora ; each attempt he makes sends her farther away from him ; she cannot understand how, proved too weak to stand alone, she is yet considered strong enough to have leaners on her shoulders ; she thinks she perceives that all he wants is some one to help him with his life work, not some one to love ; he is married already to his social theory, and she has no wish to be the handmaid of a lawful spouse ; she objects that he does not consider her individuality at all, but takes it for granted that a woman's work must be the same as her husband's whether she be fitted for it or not.   In her case there is an especial fitness for art instead of economics.   Furthermore, in her opinion, art is as much needed for the uplifting of humanity as social reform.

Thus she dismisses her lover, a good deal moved, but sure she did not love him, though not sure but she might have loved him if he had truly loved her, and that under such circumstances she might have been happier than she now finds herself.   Nevertheless, she is satisfied that her answer at the time was right.

Her aunt coming upon the two talking learns, much to her indignation, that Aurora has refused Romney.   She tells Aurora something she did not know, namely, that she is a dowerless orphan, her father having lost any inheritance for his child through marrying an Italian.   Since there was a clause in the entail excluding offspring by a foreign wife, and the property would therefore all be Romney's, his father had written to Aurora's father to ask his baby daughter for Romney.   This argument, as might be expected, only settles Aurora more determinedly than ever against Romney. In spite of this the aunt declares Aurora loves him, at which Aurora blushes in a give-away manner, though she declares it was not for love of Romney. To her indignant repudiation of the suspicion that she loves Romney her aunt retorts she will give her another month for her final answer.

A note from Romney the same day urges his love, and declares she shall be free to write women's verses, etc., but Aurora remains firm in her decision.

After this she finds herself in the unpleasant position of being constantly watched by everybody, all being interested in trying to discover the secrets of her heart. This goes on for six weeks, when suddenly her aunt dies. She was found in the morning in the chair beside the bed with an unopened letter ·in her hand. On the funeral day the cousins meet again and as Aurora is about to take the carriage to the station, Romney stops her to tell her that her aunt's will leaves her all her personal goods and funded moneys. He explains that the aunt died possessed of more than the three hundred pounds she already knew of ; in fact, there is besides thirty thousand pounds. Aurora's suspicions are immediately aroused ; she questions Romney and pushes her point until she discovers that the thirty thousand pounds had been given to her aunt by Romney in order that it might be left to her. But it turns out that the offer of this gift was in the letter which the aunt held unopened in her hand when she died, so the gift had never been accepted, and Aurora, taking advantage of that fact, tears the letter up, thus refusing what she insists upon considering bounty from her cousin.

The disappointed Romney humbly asks if he may know where she is going ; she tells him to London, and she asks him what he is going to do ; he tells her he has his work, and so with sadness and kind words they separate.

Line 38. *I choose no bay*: sweet bay or *Laurus nobilis*, formerly called laurel, the fruit only being named bayes,

from the French *baie,* a berry.   Apollo, the god of
poetry, was decorated with laurel.   The victorious both in
wars and in games were crowned with laurel.

Line 40.   *Nor myrtle — which means chiefly love* : according to the myth the mother, father, and brothers of Myrene,
a beautiful Greek girl, were murdered by robbers, and she
was carried off by them.   She escaped, however, and
became a priestess of Venus.   A lover came upon the
scene, and promised, if Myrene would give him her
hand, he would bring to justice the murderers of her
family, whose hiding place Myrene had discovered.
Venus, offended at the defection of her favorite priestess,
caused the bridegroom to expire suddenly, and changed
the bride into a myrtle, which she ordered should remain
green and odoriferous throughout the year as a proof of
her affection.   Thus myrtle was considered sacred to
Venus, and was reputed to be capable of both creating
and preserving love.   Both the Greeks and the Romans
considered it symbolic of love.

52.   *As twist about a thyrsus* : the staff carried by
Bacchus was called a thyrsus.   It was twisted with ivy,
the plant sacred to Bacchus, and surmounted by a pine
cone.

61.   *Caryatid* : a female figure with arms upraised,
used as a supporting column.

83.   *The Oread in it has a Naiad's heart And pines
for waters* : the Oread is a tree nymph and leaned down
to the water as if it were a naiad or water nymph.

140.   *Baldaquins* : originally canopies of rich silk carried
over the host (sacrament), but used in architecture to
designate a canopy over the altar.   The name comes
from Baldach (Bagdad), the city in Turkish Asia whence
the rich silks come.

151.   *Minnow gods, nymphs here and tritons there* :
nymphs were inferior goddesses either of the earth or the
water.   They dwelt in groves, on the summits of mountains, in rivers, streams, glens, and grottoes.   Tritons
were inferior marine deities, who served other marine

deities in riding over the sea. They are described by
Pausanias as having green hair on their heads, very fine and
hard scales, breathing-organs below their ears, a human
nose, a broad mouth with the teeth of animals, sea-green
eyes, hands rough like the surface of a shell, and instead
of feet a tail like that of dolphins. They are used here
as a type of any small or "minnow" divinity such as
in polytheistic stages of civilization were constantly being
added to the Pantheon as presiding deities over fresh
realms of nature.

Line 171. *When Egypt's slain, I say, let Miriam sing:*
allusion to the Song of Miriam after Pharaoh and his horsemen and chariots had been drowned in the sea. (See
Exodus xv., 19–21.) Romney considers that evil must
be dealt with before any one should take time for the cultivation of art or the beautiful.

172. *Before — where's Moses:* instead of devoting one's
self to art, a leader should be looked for to lead the
people as Moses did the Israelites, out of the bondage of
sin and poverty.

176. *Such sounding brass:* used in a passage in I. Co-
rinthians (xiii., 1.), to indicate the futility of all gifts —
knowledge, wisdom, prophecy, etc. — unless charity goes
with them.

202. *Silks from Tarsus:* Tarsus was an important city
of Asia Minor, distinguished as a commercial centre, and
hence for its great wealth. The phrase here used is
meant, of course, that with the luxuries of civilization
have come terrible evils.

209. *Show me a tear Wet as Cordelia's: "Lear.* Do
not laugh at me ; for as I am a man, I think this lady
to be my child, Cordelia. . . . Be your tears wet ?
Yes, faith. I pray, weep not." (See "King Lear,"
iv., 7, 71.) Cordelia's grief was entirely personal.
Romney, with the bias which colors so many manly ut-
terances in regard to women, deduces from a single example the generalization that women are only capable of
feeling sympathy on a personal basis.

Line 277. *But just the rich man and just Lazarus, etc.* : a somewhat exaggerated presentation of the modern problem of the rich and the poor, though true in its implication that there is suffering for both.   (See Luke xvi., 19–26.)

298. *Mastodons* : extinct animals resembling the elephant.   Their remains are found in the temperate parts of both hemispheres.

413. *Do I look a Hagar, think you ?*   Genesis xvi.

449. *They pick much oakum* : oakum is the tangled mass of fibres made by untwisting strands of rope, and used for calking seams between the planks of boats.   It is a well-known occupation of prisoners in jail, and is evidently instanced by the poet as the most humble occupation she could think of.

474. *We'll not barter, sir, The beautiful for barley* : an expressive way of saying that the soul needs nourishment through art as much as the body needs nourishment through food.

483-485. *Ah, your Fouriers failed Because not poets enough to understand That life develops from within* : Fourier (1772–1837), one of the most celebrated Socialist writers, proposed in his work " Théories des Quatres Mouvements " a scheme of society more or less mechanical.   Society was to be divided into departments called phalanges, numbering about sixteen hundred persons, who were to live in a common building, with a certain portion of land allotted to it for cultivation.   These buildings were to be made on a uniform plan, and the domestic arrangements laid down very elaborately.   The staple industry of the phalange was to be agriculture.   Out of the common gain a certain portion was to be deducted as a minimum of subsistence for each one, and the remainder divided as follows : five-twelfths to labor, four-twelfths to capital, and three-twelfths to talent.   The poet would naturally feel that society would be more or less muzzled by such a system, and growth from within kept in check.

Line 671. *O sweet my father's sister :* a form of expression found in Shakespeare and other English writers.

679. *His altar-horns :* the horns were the most sacred part of the altar among the ancient Jews. How they originated is uncertain. In the famous altar of Teima the horns sprang from the corners of the altar and were shaped like those of an ox.

779. *Male Iphigenia bound At a fatal Aulis :* Iphigenia, the daughter of Agamemnon and Clytemnestra, was about to be sacrificed by her father at Aulis, when Artemis, taking pity upon her, carried her in a cloud to Taurus, where she was made to serve the goddess as a priestess. According to the myth, Agamemnon had offended Artemis either because he had killed a stag, or boasted he was as good a shot as Artemis, or else because he failed to carry out a vow that he would sacrifice the most beautiful thing the year produced to her. In consequence of this, the Greek fleet upon the eve of its departure for Troy was becalmed at Aulis. Either the seer Calchas or the Delphic oracle declared that the only way to appease Artemis would be to sacrifice Iphigenia. Agamemnon at first objected, but finally gave way to the entreaties of Menelaus, and she was escorted to Aulis by Odysseus and Diomedes on the supposition that she was to be married to Achilles. (See Euripides, " Iphigenia at Aulis.")

793. *While I stood dumb as Griseld :* Griseld or Griselda is the type of a patient and long-suffering wife. Her story is told by Chaucer in his " Clerk of Oxenford's Tale," having been derived by him from Boccaccio's " Decameron " and from Petrarch. About the middle of the sixteenth century a song of Patient Grissel and a prose history appeared.

795. *Ragged schools :* at the time when Mrs. Browning was writing, education for the mass of the people in England was very illy provided for, there being about eight millions who could not read or write, and the establishment

of Ragged schools or schools for the poor was undertaken
by private enterprise.

Line 811. *As when the Spanish monarch crowned the
bones Of his dead love* : history relates that Pedro the cruel
of Spain, after the death of his wife, Blanche de Bourbon,
whom he treated with great cruelty, and who was finally poi-
soned, and also the death of his mistress, Maria da Padilla,
convoked a cortes and declared that Maria had been his
lawful wife and that for this reason alone he had refused
to live with Blanche. Three of the king's creatures were
brought forward who swore on the holy gospels that they
had been present at the wedding, and the cortes, though
far from convinced of the fact, declared Maria the queen
and her son Alfonso the heir of the kingdom. The story
which fits the allusion better, however, is told of Pedro I.,
King of Portugal. He married clandestinely Inez de
Castro, having been, for political reasons, contracted to a
Spanish princess. Three years after Inez was murdered
by order of her father-in-law. When Pedro came to
the throne shortly afterwards he had the body of Inez
taken from the grave, placed upon a magnificent throne,
arrayed in robes of royalty, and crowned Queen of Portugal. The court was then summoned and compelled to
do her homage as if she were a living queen. One flesh-
less hand held the sceptre, and the other the orb of
royalty. The night after the coronation there was a
grand funeral cortège extending for many miles, each
person carrying a torch. They escorted the crowned
queen, as she lay in her rich robes in a chariot drawn
by black mules, to the royal abbey of Alcobaça for
interment. Her monument is still to be seen there with
Don Pedro at the foot. The poet evidently confused
the two Pedros.

814. *Those Olympian crowns :* a reference to the
crowns which the victors in the Olympic games received.
They were simple wreaths of wild olive. These games
were celebrated every four years at Olympia in Elis, and
consisted of various contests of strength and skill. To

be victor in them was to attain the greatest possible distinction.

Line 818. *Sweet Chaldean, you read My meaning backward like your eastern books:* the name " Chaldæan " was applied originally to the inhabitants of Chaldæa, but afterwards it was applied to those men among the Assyrians who were distinguished for wisdom. They were classed as magicians, astrologers, and prophets. They were also great astronomers and were the first to calculate eclipses of the sun and moon. Their language was related to the Hebrew and read from right to left, or backwards, as we should say.

853.   *Siste, viator :* pause, traveller.

864.   *Like the sucking asp To Cleopatra's breast :* Cleopatra (69–30 B.C.), daughter of Ptolemy Auletos, celebrated for her irresistible charm, and the mistress of two great Romans, first Cæsar and then Antony, whom she fascinated when she met him in her twenty-eighth year at Tarsus in Asia Minor. Antony's life with her afterwards in Egypt brought on the war of Augustus against Cleopatra, and it is said that Augustus promised she should retain her kingdom if she would make away with Antony. At any rate, she had it announced to Antony that she was dead, having fled to her half-finished mausoleum, and Antony, overcome with grief, followed thither and died in her arms. Augustus, however, declared she should be taken captive to Rome, and she killed herself by means of an asp which she allowed to sting her.

870.   *Commination :* a threat or threatening.

898.   *Who stands upon the sea and earth and swears Time shall be nevermore:* see Revelation x., 1–6.

939.   *Nor, though the stars were suns and overburned Their spheric limitations, etc.:* the picture here called up is of the sun as it is seen during a total eclipse, with huge flames darting out into space from its burning atmosphere.

961.   *Babylon or Baalbec:* two magnificent ancient cities, of which only ruins now remain ; the first, the

chief city of Babylonia, was on the Euphrates, and is said
by some to have been founded by Semiramis; the second
was a large and splendid city of Syria. The poet uses
these cities here as symbols of the intellectual structures
she will rear in the wide desert of her newly gained freedom.

Line 1021. *Logarithm*: a kind of auxiliary number devised by Napier to abridge arithmetical calculations. The
relations of the logarithms to common numbers are those
of numbers in an arithmetical series to correspond with
those in a geometrical series, so that by the additions
and subtractions of the former multiplications and divisions
of the latter are obtained.

1037. *Doit*: a small Dutch coin, also used in Scotland,
and on account of its insignificance used to denote anything of little or no value.

1095. *Cruel springe*: a trap in the form of a noose,
which is fastened to an elastic body and drawn close
with a sudden spring.

1149–1151. *King Solomon Considered, when he wore his
holy ring Charactered over with the ineffable spell*: Solomon, according to the Rabbins, had a magical ring in
which was set a chased stone that told the king everything
he wished to know.

1166. *Valdarno*: Val d'Arno, the name given to the
country through which the river Arno flows just before it
turns to the west and flows through Florence.

Third Book. In this we find Aurora after seven years
of literary work in London. .She is about to spend the
evening writing, and dismissing her maid rather crossly,
proceeds to open her letters. From her remarks as she
reads them it appears that she has gained some popularity in her chosen career, and has come into sufficient
prominence to have many and various criticisms hurled at
her. The last letter opened is from Vincent Carrington,
who wants her advice as to a picture of Danaë, and asks
if she has heard anything of Romney .

The mention of Romney takes her back to the day

they parted, and recalls to her mind the course of her life since then : how she had taken a room up three flights of stairs in Kensington, how she had received inspiration from watching the play of sunlight and fog over the London roofs, how she had written excellent things indifferently, and bad things excellently, and been praised especially for the latter, how youths and maidens showered their appreciative letters upon her until she woke up to the fact that she was becoming popular, and then realizes that she has so far merely been playing with art.

Yet she feels that she has the right stuff in her, and henceforth sets herself to work more seriously, although obliged to give part of her time to the booksellers at reviewing and hack work of various sorts, in order to supply the necessities of her life. Her next book, though it did not please the critics as well as her earlier work, pleased herself much better, for she knew that, in spite of faults, she had really put her heart and soul into it.

Just at this time she is surprised by a visit from a stranger, Lady Waldemar, who she soon learns had climbed her three flights of stairs to her lodging to confess to her that she is in love with her cousin Romney Leigh, and that Romney, in accordance with his views in regard to bridging over the chasm between the rich and the poor, is about to marry a poor girl of the people.

Lady Waldemar describes how she has interested herself in Romney's schemes for reform, read socialistic literature, and subscribed money, all with the idea of making an impression upon him, but to no purpose ; and now, in order to gain time, she has persuaded Romney to put his wedding off for a month, by representing to him that in order to give it its proper weight as a social reform it should have the sanction of his kin. She therefore proposes to take Aurora to see his intended bride, Marian Erle, so by "their presence to raise the wedding up from its doubtful place."

Aurora, who has all through shown her dislike of Lady Waldemar's tactics, confesses she does not see how this

is going to better Lady Waldemar's prospects, but Lady
Waldemar explains that she expects Aurora, after she
has seen the girl, to dissuade Romney from marrying
her.   Aurora declares she has no power nor wish to
break the match, and Lady Waldemar goes off in high
displeasure.

Two hours after Aurora seeks out Marian Erle in her
dingy quarters in a desperate neighborhood.   After describing Marian Erle's appearance, she relates her story,
not as Marian told it, but in her own passionate words.
Marian was born upon the ledge of the Malvern hills, her
father a worker at random jobs, who drank and cursed
his wife when there were no more pence for drink, her
mother beating her in revenge for her own bad treatment.
Marian, however, was an unusual child.   She crept away
from home through the fields of gorse to gaze up at the
sky, from which she gained more civilizing influences than
she did from Sunday-school later.   At Sunday-school,
however, she knew one little girl she loved, Rose, who
had become bad since, and here also, in learning about
God, she realized more and more with anguish the
degradation of her father and mother.

Her parents used to take her with them when they
went on their tramps, and she had seen towns and fairs,
once Manchester and once the sea.   Thus she lived and
learned, people being kind to her, and pedlers, when they
found she could read, tossing her from their packs some
mutilated volume, from which she chose the good things,
while the bad things she tore into bits so that none might
read them.   Her parents did not find this child, whose
pleasure was to think of rhymes from her small stock of
poems, very satisfactory, for out-door jobs went ill with
her, and household work she was not born to, yet she
earned something knitting hose and darning stockings.
If her parents had stayed in the North they might have
got something out of her in factory work, but as it was
they could only tramp with her.   Finally, one day her
mother sold her to a neighboring squire, and the poor

child, horrified and disgusted, escaped from under their hands, and, strengthened by fear, ran over the fields and the uplands until she fell fainting into a ditch. Later she was found by a wagoner who carried her to a hospital in a distant town. She lay there for many weeks in a fever, but finally recovered and was told that she was free to go next week. She was in despair as to where she was to go, when, the day before her last day, Romney came through the hospital, and asked her where she was going. She replied by telling him something of her story, and that she presumed she would be lost like her father and mother, as she did not know where she was going. Romney sympathized with her and comforted her, and found her a place in a famous seamstress' house, and there she had sewed and sewed, wondering all the while if Romney would remember her when they met after death.

Line 3. *" Others shall gird thee . . . to go Where thou wouldst not "* : " Verily, verily, I say unto thee, when thou wast young, thou girdedst thyself, and walkedst whither thou wouldest : but when thou shalt be old, thou shalt stretch forth thy hands, and another shall gird thee, and carry *thee* whither thou wouldest not." (John xxi., 18.)

11. *Have mislaid the keys of heaven and earth :* see Matthew xvi., 19.

48. *If but one angel spoke from Ararat :* Ararat was a mountainous region in Armenia where the Ark rested after the flood, and where God spoke to Noah. Hence used by the poet to indicate a region whence divine guidance might come.

54. *And signs " Elisha to you "* : referring to Elijah's mantle which fell from him when he was translated to heaven in a chariot of fire, and which Elisha picked up and with it accomplished the same wonder as Elijah had. (See II. Kings ii., 1–15.)

78. *My critic Stokes :* Robert Browning uses the same fanciful name with others to designate imitative poets, in his little poem " Popularity," stanza xii. (Vol. iv., *Camberwell Browning.*)

Line 86. *All true poets laugh unquenchably Like Shake-speare and the gods:* an allusion to Shakespeare's inimitable humor and to the passage in Homer which describes the inextinguishable laughter of the gods. ("Odyssey," Book viii.)

88-90. *Dante smiled With such a needy heart on two pale lips, We cry "Weep rather, Dante":* Dante is a good example of a great poet whose temper is always more or less solemn and serious.

98. *A ninth seal:* a facetious allusion based upon the account in Revelation of the book closed with seven seals, at the opening of each of which direful things happened. (See Revelation v., vi., vii., and viii.)

108. *Phalansteries:* associations formed according to a plan suggested by the socialist Fourier. The members lived in a dwelling common to all, making common stock of their capital and labor, and sharing the results according to their several investments. Used here as a general term to indicate Romney's schemes for the welfare of the people.

122. *Danaë:* the beautiful daughter of Acrisius. An oracle having prophesied that a son of hers would be the means of his grandfather's death, she was shut up in an underground room, but Jupiter penetrated it in the form of a shower of gold and wooed her, and their son Perseus fulfilled the prophecy.

172. *Like some Druidic idol's fiery brass:* it is said that the Druids often indulged in human sacrifices. Accord-ing to the authorities on the subject, they used to make huge images of straw, the limbs of which were joined together and shaped by wicker-work. These images they filled with human beings, wild beasts, and wood for fuel, and then set fire to them. Information in regard to the Druids is not, however, considered altogether trust-worthy, and as likely as not some old writer may have described them as using idols of brass, such as the poet alludes to, in the way above described, though we have not met with any mention of brass idols.

Line 190.   *No one sings, Descending Sinai:* the mountain where Moses received the ten commandments, a striking way of saying that awe-inspiring spectacles do not inspire one to poetical creation.

191.   *On Parnassus mount You take a mule to climb and not a muse, etc.* : Parnassus, being the mountain sacred to Apollo, stands for the fountain-head of poetry, but if the poet seeks to climb thither he will find himself upon a mule instead of a muse. Similarly, nature furnishes no inspiration. The great city alone kindles the poetic spark. In other words, the modern poet must get his inspiration from the seething human life around him rather than from the contemplation of religion symbolized in "Sinai;" from classical sources symbolized in "Parnassus;" or from nature.

197.   *Like Pharaoh's armaments in the deep Red Sea:* Exodus xv., 19–21.

202.   *And you and Israel's other singing girls, Ay, Miriam with them:* Exodus xv., 19–21.

218.   *Collegisse juvat:* it is profitable to have come together.

252.   *Like those hot fire-seeds of creation held In Jove's clenched palm before the worlds were sown:* Zeus, not being the oldest of the gods, cannot properly be spoken of as holding the seeds of creation in his hands, for according to the Hesiodic Theogony the Earth and the Heavens and various other cosmic powers came into existence before Zeus, who was himself the son of Rhea and Cronos. Yet even in Hesiod he is spoken of as the sire of gods and men, and according to some legends Zeus is said to have animated men and animals with heavenly fire, after they had been moulded out of clay by Prometheus.

323.   *Champagne:* a province in France where the celebrated champagne wine is made.

324.   *Nephelococcygia:* Cloud-cuckoo-town ; the town built by the birds in Aristophanes's comedy of "The Birds."

Line 391.   *I meet my lion simply as Androcles :* Androcles was a runaway slave who took refuge in a cavern. A lion soon entered, but instead of tearing him to pieces, lifted up his fore-paw, in which was a thorn, so that Androcles might take it out. Afterwards the slave was captured and doomed to fight a lion in the Roman arena. It happened that the same lion was let out against him, and recognizing his benefactor showed toward him every demonstration of love and gratitude. This story is told in Æsop's Fables and the Gesta Romanorum, but comes originally from Aulus Gellius on the authority of Plistonices.

431.   *Mayfair :* the section of London east of Hyde Park between Bond street and Park lane, where the houses belonging to the *beau monde* cluster. Mayfair especially, with Belgravia towards the south, and Tyburnia to the north, of the West End, make up the part of town in the neighborhood of Hyde Park where the gentility and wealth of Vanity Fair keep their booths.

459.   *Blowsalinda :* a country girl in Gay's comedy, "The Shepherd's Week," which portrays the rudeness and poverty of pastoral life.

460.   *Lyons velvet :* made in the town of Lyons in France.

471.   *Germane Wertherism :* Goethe's famous book, "The Sorrows of Werther," is a type of the intensely romantic, so would, as Lady Waldemar hints, be germane to her feelings at the time.

472.   *Champs Elysées :* the pleasure promenade of Paris for walking, driving, riding, and watching others do so of all sorts and conditions of life. It runs from the Place de la Concorde to the triumphal arch, the Arc de l'Étoile, whence avenues branch out to the Parisian park, — the Bois de Boulogne.

473.   *A ghost, and sighing like Dido's :* in the sixth book of Virgil's "Æneid," Æneas meets the ghost of Dido in Hades, where she had been driven by love of him ; for

when Æneas left her she committed suicide by killing herself with his sword.

Line 514. *The Genius of the Vatican :* the famous antique fragment, sculptured by Apollonius, in which Michael Angelo is said to have found the secret of his inspiration in representing the human form. In his blind old age he had himself led up to it that he might feel it with his intelligent hands.

517. *The torso of the Dancing Faun :* the classic remnant attributed to Praxiteles.

519. *Buonarroti's mask :* refers to a significant detail in the sculpture of Michael Angelo Buonarroti's reclining figure of Night which is one of the statues belonging to the Tomb of Giuliano de Medici in the Medici Chapel in Florence. This mask is under Night's arm, on which she is resting, and it represents a rude, strong, swinish face with lip pushed forward like a boar's snout, the mustaches flowing back on either side, and two strong teeth protruding in front.

546. *Equal scorn of triangles and wine :* a way of saying he cared neither for mathematics nor for the convivial life of the college.

548. *Lost count of Homer's ships :* Homer's catalogue of the Greek ships that went to the Trojan war, in the second book of the "Iliad."

549. *Melbourne's poor-bills :* these bills were intended to suppress indiscriminate alms-giving, pauperism having at that time reached alarming proportions in England. They were passed under Melbourne's ministry, though he himself was not distinguished for his eagerness for reform. — *Ashley's factory bills :* these were introduced by Lord Ashley in 1833 and a factory act was passed prohibiting the labor of children under ten years of age, limiting the working day to eight hours for children under fourteen, providing for school attendance and for medical care. Mrs. Browning's poem "The Cry of the Children" was instrumental in the passage of this bill.

550. *Aspasia :* this celebrated intellectual woman of

Athens, the friend and comrade of Pericles, has been admired in spite of a relation which is not according to the ideals of modern society.

Line 555. *Dead Cæsar who 'stops bungholes' in the cask:* "To what base uses we may return, Horatio ! Why may not imagination trace the noble dust of Alexander, till he find it stopping a bunghole ? " ("Hamlet," v., i., 223.) It will be remembered that Shakespeare refers to Alexander as a Cæsar.

584. *Fourier:* (1772–1837) the originator of a system of communism called Fourierism or Phalansterianism, which has influenced, more or less, subsequent socialistic movements. (See preceding note, line 108.)

585. *Proudhon:* (1809–1865) wrote on the "Solution of the Social Problem," and astonished society by declaring that "All property is robbery." — *Considérant:* Victor-Prosper, born 1805, son of Jean-Baptiste Considérant, and an enthusiastic disciple of Fourier. He founded *La Phalange,* a journal of social science, in 1836, to expound Fourierism. — *Louis Blanc:* (1803–1845) wrote a work in 1840 on the "Organization of Labor," which advanced the opinion that men should labor for the community rather than for themselves, and that they should be remunerated in accordance with their wants by a central government under a chosen administration.

596. *Sue:* Eugène (1801–1857), French novel writer, who is most popularly known by his work "The Wandering Jew." His book on "The Mysteries of Paris," in which he describes the proletariat as Gauls and the capitalists as Frank invaders, probably gave him his place on Lady Waldemar's table with other literature on social regeneration.

601. *Ten hours' movement:* in 1847 the Ten Hours' Act introduced by Mr. Fielden brought much relief to the factory workers.

603. *Unmoved as the Indian tortoise 'neath the world:* in Hindu mythology the world is said to rest on a great tortoise, swimming in the primeval ocean.

Line 706. *Medicean Venus :* said to be a copy of a masterpiece of Praxiteles, the Venus of Cnidos. It was in the
possession of the Medici in Florence when it first attracted
attention about two hundred years ago. On the base of
it is an inscription attributing it to an Athenian sculptor
of 200 B.C., Cleomenes, but its authenticity is doubtful.

831. *Malvern Hill :* in Herefordshire, and well known
to the poet, whose early youth was spent at Hope End in
the neighborhood. (See Biographical Introduction in
Vol. I. of this edition.)

884. *Golden walls of gorse :* a prickly plant with
golden blossoms growing wild on English hillsides.

949. *Manchester :* the great manufacturing centre of
England, situated on the Irwell thirty-one miles east of
Liverpool.

974. *A Thomson's Seasons, mulcted of the Spring :*
James Thomson (1700–1748), one of the first of the
British poets to return to nature for his inspiration. His
first work, "The Seasons," gained and still merits appreciation for its genuine love of nature and charm of
language in spite of some pompousness.

981. *From Churchyard Elegies :* Gray's "Elegy
written in a Country Churchyard," published in 1751,
after several years of revision. As Byron says of it, "It
pleased instantly and eternally."— *Edens Lost :* Milton's
"Paradise Lost."

982. *Burns :* Robert (1759–1796), Scotland's promise
of a great poet of whom a recent critic says, "Such a
singing faculty — such a sweep of pathos and passion —
so genuine a power of humor and satire will not soon
appear again. Alas! that he, too, must be added to the
cut short lives — the 'inheritors of unfulfilled renown.' "
— *Bunyan :* John (1628–1688), whose "Pilgrim's Progress" is one of the great books of the world, winning its
way to the religious class for which it was intended by
its vivid portrayal of their ideals, and to the great world
of readers by its artistic power. — *Selkirk :* Alexander
(born 1676), the Scotch adventurer who, for quarrel-

ling with his commander was set ashore on the island of
Juan Fernandez with a few necessaries, a fowling-piece,
gunpowder, and shot.   He lived alone here for four years
and four months, and was rescued by Capt. Woods Rogers.
It is said that De Foe got the main points for his story of
" Robinson Crusoe " from Selkirk's papers giving his experience while on the island. — *Tom Jones :* Henry Field-
ing's celebrated novel.

Line 1053.   *Stertorous :* snoring.

1207.   *Weep where John was laid while Jesus loved
him :* see John xiii., 23.

1222.   *As the ointment-box broke on the Holy feet To let
out the rich medicative nard :* see Luke vii., 37–39.
Nard or spikenard is made from a famous medicinal herb
found in Nepal.   The roots contain a highly odoriferous
oil, which is used either in a liquid, oily form or is
rubbed up with fat into an ointment.

Fourth Book.   In this book the story of Marian Erle is
continued.   Among the workers in the establishment
where she sewed was one poor girl, Lucy Gresham, who
was ill with consumption, and who finally dropped down
suddenly in the street one day and was carried home to
die.

When Marian heard this she immediately gave up her
position and went to nurse Lucy, regardless of her own
loss of work.   And after Lucy's death she nursed her
bed-ridden, thankless grandmother until she also died.
While here she again met Romney, and was pleased to
find he was not displeased that she had left her work to
perform these last offices for this wretched pair.   When
her work there was finished he had spoken to her and
proposed that they two should not wait until death should
make them equal, but should join together now in a
protest against the wrongs of society, which makes so
great a gap between the rich privileged classes and the
poor.   They two had both been drawn beyond themselves to minister unto others, he through knowledge,
she through feeling, both leaving their several vantage

posts to do it, and since he had found her, he would take it as a sign that he should ask her to be his wife and fellow-worker.

To Aurora's question, "So indeed he loves you?" Marian looks up wonderingly, and replies, "He loves all, and me, of course." Aurora philosophizes with some sarcasm over this reply of Marian's, wondering whether that is indeed love which simply includes one in a perfect round of love, and whether Marian's satisfaction with it is not better than the haggling over so much love for so much which her class indulges in. She concludes that if marriage is a contract the love should be equal on both sides, but if a mere religion, right on the part of the bride to give is evidently all that is required.

Marian expresses a doubt as to whether Aurora thinks her worthy of Romney and, after a pretty speech from Aurora, goes on to vindicate his choice of her, and tell how she will in her unselfish thought for him make him a better wife, perhaps, than one of the beautiful ladies, who, in delight at their own beauty, forget the poor sewing-girls toiling to make them beautiful, and would also forget him in the contemplation of their own beauty.

Just here Romney is discovered to be in the room. Aurora explains how and why she came, and after the usual fencing with him tells him she is pleased with his bride if he is. She thinks the old portraits of the Leighs will be glad to own this good true Marian, as she also will be, for even half-poets are always true democrats, and she comprehends and justifies his choice. He retorts that she cannot comprehend his motives, but he accepts her favorable thoughts of Marian. He considers that they have fallen upon days when mutual love is less needed than common love to be extended toward the many. The love the poets talk about is out of date in his estimation. Aurora, irritated at Romney's unemotional way of regarding life, impulsively kisses Marian, who has more of the freshness of nature than he has with his theories, and, as she leaves, asks if Marian can be married

from her house.   But Romney, of course, refuses this,
for in order that his marriage may have its full effect,
Marian must come to him direct from the people.   He
follows Aurora downstairs after this interview and walks
home with her.   Their talk, on the way, is about the
ordinary events of the day, while they are conscious of an
undercurrent of reality which they are feverishly eager to
avoid, — not of a reality that would lead them to agree-
ment, but of one which would take them far asunder.
The strange sound of Romney's voice as he said "Good
night" haunts Aurora with a sense of impending trouble
all night.

During the month which passes between this and the
wedding Aurora does nothing more for Marian, for which
she greatly reproaches herself, hinting that she might have
prevented subsequent events if she had truly interested
herself in Marian's welfare, had told Romney of Lady
Waldemar's designs, and had realized that the love of
such a woman as Lady Waldemar would simply be a
readjustment of self-love, and that in the attainment of her
desire she would be utterly unscrupulous.

The day of the wedding at last arrives, and Aurora
gives a vivid description of the guests, commingled of
aristocrats and the poor.   Scraps of conversation fall
from the former, revealing their frivolous interests, and
the fact that the event itself will have no further effect
than to make them think Romney a crank or a lunatic.
Even Lord Howe, whom Aurora describes as brought up
a radical and socialist, though he hardly practises his
principles, has nothing but criticism for Romney, first on
the score that in marrying Marian Erle he is not being
true to the only true thing on earth, love, but is acting a
play with it ; and second, that what he wants to preach
by this play, namely, the filling up of the ditches between
the classes, will be impossible of accomplishment, for they
have become so widely separated that they can never come
together again.

During the talk references are made to the fact of the

bride's lateness, when suddenly there is a commotion and
Romney appears on the top stair of the altar with white
face, and announces there will be no marriage, his bride
having left him, and bids the guests go and feast themselves according to the programme.

There is silence for a moment in the church, and then
comes an uproar from the disappointed mob, which ac-
cuses Romney of trickery, and works itself up to such a
pitch of rage that it shrieks out for Romney to be killed.
Aurora stretches out her arms toward him in a vain
impulse to save him, and feeling herself drawn back by
some one, faints away.

Afterwards Lord Howe told her that the tumult was
quelled by the police, and from Romney she receives
Marian's letter, which gives up Romney in pitiful and
affecting terms, declaring that he is too far above her and
confessing that she is not what he thought her, but a
light girl who will be happier living as she intends to do
than she would be as his wife.

Romney and Aurora ponder and conjecture over
Marian's letter, but can come to no satisfactory conclu-
sions as to the cause of her action.   Aurora thinks of
Lady Waldemar, and tries to hint to Romney that a
certain friend of his had reasons of her own for throwing
back the match, but he repels her, and goes on to say
that he has discovered that another woman besides Lady
Waldemar and Aurora had visited Marian.   Aurora asks
him if he had never heard of Rose, a ruined creature.
When he hears this, he blames himself for not having
been more of a real friend to Marian, who had never
mentioned Rose to him, and is tortured by the thought of
her contamination.   Aurora, however, tries to reassure
him that whatever may have happened to Marian, she is
sure that she keeps pure in heart and aim.   But he will
not be comforted, and declares it was a sad day for
Marian when she chanced on his philanthropy, which
far from being able to take a world on its shoulders had
not been able to save one child's soul.

Aurora tries to comfort him, and he is so touched by
her kindness that he concludes the printers' devils have
not spoiled her heart, and that perhaps she was not so
wrong years ago when she insisted on writing her poems,
for she at least has ruined no one, has even helped youth
to live its day with innocent distraction ; the little shepherd girl asleep on the mountain, her flocks going astray,
is better than the imperfectly trained sheep dog who bites
the kids through too much zeal.   This does not strike
Aurora as being a very good comparison, and she asks
him if she looks as if she had slept, for though she is two
years younger than he, and he has had all the turmoil of
life among men, she looks more worn out than he.   But
though Aurora puts in a word for art, he still refuses to
regard art as a serious occupation in life, and reiterates his
conviction that the only thing that is worth while is the pursuit of helping starving or freezing humanity.   He ends
by wishing he might have had her heart, but that is past
now.   He thanks her for her kindness to him, and tells
her to sing her songs if she will, but to reflect that if art
be indeed the higher life, for the sake of that she must
live the lower human life.   Thus they part, Aurora
feeling that she cannot but respect him, but evidently hurt
that he has no comprehension of the needs and aspirations
of her artistic temperament.

Line 147.   *Putting out his hand to touch this ark:* see II.
Samuel vi., 6, 7.

190.   *Rialto-prices:* the Rialto was the commercial
centre of Venice, hence "Rialto-prices" is equivalent to
"market value."

196.   *To mount the pile as Indian widows do:* refers
to the custom in India of widows immolating themselves
on the funeral pyre of their husbands.

307.   *An obolus inscribed With Cæsar's image lightly:*
the obolus was originally a Greek silver coin, later struck
in bronze, a head on one side, an owl on the other, of the
weight and value of one-sixth drachma.   It was used in
the Middle Ages in Hungary, Poland, and Bohemia, and

later in France, so it is likely to have been used also as a Roman coin, as the poet here seems to take for granted.

Line 309. *Sublime Vandykes:* Vandyke (1599–1641), Dutch painter, famous for his portraits of royal and noble personages. He did his best work in England when he was employed by Charles I.

340. *Set a swan To swim the Trenton:* apparently a reference to the Trenton Falls of Oneida County, New York. The stream on which they are, Canada creek, is famous as having a fall of three hundred and twelve feet in two miles. The wild turbulence its six cataracts make would not afford the placid pool-like surface befitting the swimming of a swan.

370. *As Austria's daughter to imperial France, etc.:* reference to Marie Louise, the Austrian princess whom Napoleon I. married for his second wife.

373. *Saint James's:* the church of St. James's square, built by Wren in 1682, on the south side of Piccadilly, in a neighborhood of rank and fashion.

379. *Tragic masks:* worn by the actors on the ancient Greek stage.

380. *Cothurn:* high buskins worn by Greek actors to increase their height.

383. *Athenian wives Who shrieked in fits at the Eumenides:* the story goes that when the " Eumenides " of Æschylus was acted at Athens the aspect of the Furies in pursuit of Orestes was so terrible that the women fainted.

399. *Spanish marriage-schemes:* these marriages were that of Queen Isabella to her cousin Francis, duke of Cadiz, and of Louisa, the Queen's sister, to the Duc de Montpensier, son of Louis Philippe. All Europe was agitated over them, especially England, because it was afraid French influence would become supreme in Madrid. As it turned out, however, they did not have the political consequences looked for.

402. *Can Guizot stand:* François-Pierre Guillaume Guizot, distinguished as a writer and conservative states-

man. His political career was by no means smooth, for in 1830 he was driven from office, and later when he was minister of foreign affairs he was obliged to flee from France upon the abdication of Louis Philippe, in 1848.

Line 403. *Has Dickens turned his hinge A-pinch upon the fingers of the great:* a reference to the manner in which Dickens showed up some of the shortcomings of English society and institutions.

406. *Moly:* a magical plant among the ancients generally supposed to be a species of garlic. Homer relates in the "Odyssey" that it was given by Mercury to Odysseus as a charm to withstand the enchantments of Circe.

467. *Where we disavow Being keeper to our brother, we're his Cain:* that is, it is as bad to shirk responsibility for the welfare of a brother as it is actively to do him harm, as Cain did Abel.

482. *He once, in the first creation-week, Called creatures good:* see Genesis i., 21–25.

486-488. *In the middle age, I think they called malignant fays and imps Good people:* with the spread of Christianity, fairies which had been looked upon as good spirits came to be regarded as malignant imps.

493. *As chaste, or nearly so, as Potiphar's:* a sarcasm, of course. (See Genesis xxxix., 6–10.)

538. *Half Saint Giles in frieze:* St. Giles is one of the old city churches, built 1545, standing in Cripplegate, and giving its name to one of the poor sections of London.

539. *Saint James in cloth of gold:* that is, the well-dressed rich parish of London, whose splendor recalls that of the famous meeting of the English and French kings at Calais, henceforth called the "field of the cloth of gold." (See Shakespeare's "Henry VIII.," i., 1.)

541. *Hampstead Heath:* a popular pleasure-ground of two hundred and forty acres, long resorted to by the London public on holidays, in 1870 made a city park.

545. *Pimlico:* adjoining Belgravia, toward the West

End of London, through which in going westward Romney's poorer guests would pass.

Line 595. *On Raffael's mild Madonna of the Bird :* Madonna of the Goldfinch, in the Uffizi Palace in Florence.

657. *And puts on Mayfair manners :* see preceding book, note, line 431.

665. *Prince Albert's model lodging-house :* Prince Albert was always greatly interested in improving the condition of the poor.   In a letter to Colonel Phipps, quoted in Theodore Martin's '' Life,'' he speaks of a society that has established model lodging-houses.   These have been completed and have answered.   Though the subscriptions for the general fund are very small, those for the different lodging-houses are large and have nearly covered the expense.

667. *Cheapside :* to the east of St. Paul's, originally the market place, and still the mercantile heart and densest populated centre of London.

674. *Damiens' trunk and limbs :* Robert François Damiens (1715–1757), called Robert the Devil for his wicked exploits, finally finished his career by attempting to assassinate Louis XV.   Although the king soon recovered from his wound, Damiens was condemned as a regicide to be torn to pieces by four horses.   This sentence was executed March 28, 1757, on the Place de Grève.   Before being put to death he was tortured for one hour and a half with red-hot pincers, boiling oil, molten lead, etc.   From the roofs and windows of all the houses in the neighborhood spectators watched the scene — men and women, among whom were many ladies of rank.

712. *Goes floating, on traditions of his kind, Across the theoretic flood from France, etc. :* referring to the socialistic theories which emanated from such men as Fourier, Proudhon, Considérant, Blanc, and others.

748. *He takes it up, and dresses it, And acts a play with it, as Hamlet did :* Romney, in Lord Howe's estimation, is mad as Hamlet was said to have been, for

using love as a means of teaching the world how the gap between the classes should be filled up, as Hamlet used the play to find out whether his mother and uncle were guilty. (See "Hamlet," iii, 2.)

Line 773. *We'll liken to a brutalized King Lear, etc.*: the comparison here brings out the fact that the rich class feeds upon the inheritance of the poor, who have been denuded of what rightfully belongs to them, and that Romney's plan of marriage will be powerless to bring about any real reconciliation between the two classes, which have drifted so far apart that they cannot possibly have anything in common. The rich have forgotten that their wealth is founded upon past violence, and now regard it as their special privilege, while the poor are only concerned with their next meal.

1059. *Cairo's street*: in the swarming thoroughfare of this ancient Egyptian city the plagues of the tropics were wont to strike down their victims suddenly.

1100. *Chromatic sequence of fine thought In learned modulation*: these metaphors drawn from musical parlance finely suggest great subtlety of thought. Complicated musical effects may be gained by modulations from one key into another through chromatic progressions of chords, leading to some final harmony in a key which would be unconjectured until it was reached.

1120. *The mountains of Vaucluse*: a department in France bordered on the south and west by the Rhone and Durance rivers.

1145. *Autumn cyclamens*: ordinarily described as a spring flower.

1150. *The poet of Vaucluse*: Petrarch, who retired to this romantic spot and there poured out in poetry his passion for Laura.

1171. *Like swallows which the exasperate, dying year Sets spinning in black circles*: every one has probably observed swallows flying in this way when getting ready for their migrations to the South in the autumn.

1184. *This social Sphinx Who sits between the sepulchres* *and stews :* the Sphinx, a monster half lion, half woman, infested the high road of Thebes, propounding to travellers a riddle, and all those who had been unable to guess it she had killed, until Œdipus guessed it, when she threw herself down from the rock and perished. The poet likens Society to this devouring Sphinx, that sits between the sepulchres (death) and the stews (standing for physical and material life), mocking God. This spectacle should bring out protest from those on God's side even if they are slain for it, and if they are quiet they will suffer through their own conscience.

Line 1186. *Mow ;* a wry face.

APPENDIX.

EXTRACTS FROM CONTEMPORANEOUS REVIEWS OF
"AURORA LEIGH."

FOSTER, the essayist, has somewhere said that the person who interests us most is the one that most gives us the idea of *ample being*. Applying this remark to books, which are but persons in a transmigrated form, we discern one grand source of the profound impression produced in us by "Aurora Leigh." Other poems of our own day may have higher finish, or a higher degree of certain poetic qualities ; but no poem embraces so wide a range of thought and emotion, or takes such complete possession of our nature. Mrs. Browning is, perhaps, the first woman who has produced a work which exhibits all the peculiar powers without the negations of her sex ; which superadds to masculine vigour, breadth, and culture, feminine subtlety of perception, feminine quickness of sensibility, and feminine tenderness. It is difficult to point to a woman of genius who is not either too little feminine, or too exclusively so. But in this, her longest and greatest poem, Mrs. Browning has shown herself all the greater poet because she is intensely a poetess.

The *story* of "Aurora Leigh" has no other merit than that of offering certain elements of life, and certain situations which are peculiarly fitted to call forth the writer's rich thought and experience. It has nothing either fresh or felicitous in structure or incident ; and we are especially sorry that Mrs. Browning has added one more to the imitations of the catastrophe in " Jane Eyre," by smiting her hero with blindness before he is made happy in the love of Aurora. Life has sadness and bitterness enough for a disappointed philanthropist like Romney Leigh, short of maiming or blindness ; and the outflow of love and compassion towards physical ills is less rare in woman than complete sympathy with mental sorrows. Hence think the lavish mutilation of heroes' bodies, which has become the habit of novelists, while it happily does not represent probabilities in the present state of things, weakens instead of strengthening tragic effect ; and, as we said, we regret that Mrs. Browning has given this habit her strong sanction. Other criticisms might be passed on " Aurora Leigh," considered as a representation of incident and dialogue, but we are little inclined to spend our small space in pointing out faults which will be very slightly felt by any one who has heart and mind enough to respond to all the beautiful feeling, the large thought, and the rich melodious song of this rare poem. . . . The most striking characteristic of " Aurora Leigh," distinguishing it from the larger proportion of that contemporary poetry which wins the applause of reviewers, is, that its melody, fancy, and imagination — what we may call its poetical *body* — is everywhere informed by a *soul*, namely, by genuine thought and feeling. There is no petty striving after special effects, no heaping up of images for their own sake, no trivial play of fancy run quite astray from the control of deeper sensibility ; there is simply a full mind pouring itself out in song as its natural and easiest medium. This mind has its far-stretching thoughts, its abundant treasure of well-digested learning, its acute observation of life, its yearning sympathy with multiform human sorrow, its store of personal domestic love and joy ; and these are given out in a delightful alternation of pathos, reflection, satire playful or pungent, and picturesque description, which carries us with swifter pulses than usual through four hundred pages, and makes us sorry to find ourselves at the end.— *Westminster Review,* 1857.

MRS. BARRETT BROWNING has won for herself the first place among our female poets. Falling short of the exquisite grace characterizing the masterpieces of Felicia Hemans, without the simplicity of L. E. L., or the variety of dramatic power which distinguishes Joanna Baillie, her earlier volumes contain poems evincing a depth of thought and subtlety of expression peculiarly her own. . . . No one could fail . . to regard "Aurora Leigh"— the most mature as well as the longest of her works — that into which she says her "highest convictions upon Life and Art have entered " — with the profoundest interest and sanguine expectations.

To attempt to write a *novel,* — which shall be also a *poem,* — is a daring one. We have abandoned the absurdity of setting limits to the sphere of poetry, but there is a certain incongruity between the natural variety and expansion of the one, and the concentration required in the other. The general success of this effort is remarkable. Few volumes of verse have such intense interest. It has been found by an ingenious critic to contain more lines than "Paradise Lost" or the "Odyssey,"— yet there are few people who do not try to read it at a sitting. Once into the

vortex of the story, we are whirled on, forgetful of
criticism, of the authoress, and of ourselves. This
is a high recommendation, and has contributed largely
towards the enthusiastic reception of the work ; but
when one has leisure to be censorious, he is met by
defects equally striking. The difficulties of the design
have not been entirely surmounted. The authoress
is given to a diffusive style ; she drags us through
many pages in "Aurora Leigh" which are unneces-
sary, trifling, and wearisome. That it may become
a story, it sometimes ceases to be a poèm. Blank
verse is the most flexible, and accommodating of all
measures : it can sound, as in "The Brook," like
graceful conversation, or with the Æolian pulsation
of the "Morte d'Arthur," preserving its harmonious
fulness ; but in "Aurora Leigh" there are cases in
which Mrs. Browning has broken loose altogether
from the meshes of versification, and run riot in prose
cut up into lines of ten syllables. . . . The affectation of Originality is the next fault to the want of it.
Irregular lines, extravagant metaphors, jarring combi-
nations, are the occasional *defects*, never the *signs* of
genius. An ostentation of strength is the most infal-
lible proof of weakness. A profusion of words is no
voucher for richness of thought. Those are not the
best scholars who make the most numerous quotations
from the Greek. We know no poem so good as this,
with so many glaring offences against those first principles. Mrs. Browning's greatest failure is in her metaphors : some of them are excellent, but when they
are bad — and they are often bad — they are very
bad. By a single ugly phrase, a single hideous word,
dragged in, one would think, from the furthest ends
of the earth, she every now and then mars the har-

mony of a whole page of beauty. She sadly wants simplicity, and the calm strength that flows from it. She writes in a high fever. She is constantly introducing geographical, geological, and antiquarian references, almost always out of place, and often incorrect.[1] . . . Mrs. Browning seems at once proud and ashamed of her womanhood. She protests, not unjustly, against the practice of judging artists by their sex; but she takes the wrong means to prove her manhood. In recoil from mincing fastidiousness, she now and then becomes coarse. She will not be taxed with squeamishness, and introduces words unnecessarily, which are eschewed in the most familiar conversation. To escape the imputation of over-refinement she swears without provocation. These are grave accusations: but the authoress would be the first to disclaim the shield of the spurious gallantry which accords her sex an exemption from the full severity of legitimate censure. A few examples, taken almost at random from among many, will vindicate the justice of our remarks.

The description of a face that haunted Aurora's early years gives scope for a perfect shoal of mangled and pompous similes. It was, she says, "by turns

> " Ghost, fiend, and angel, fairy, witch, and sprite, —
> A dauntless Muse, who eyes a dreadful Fate,
> A loving Psyche who loses sight of Love,
> A still Medusa, with mild milky brows
> All curdled and all clothed upon with snakes
> Whose slime falls fast as sweat will; or anon

---

[1] Is it hypercritical to advert to the fact that the main incident in "Aurora Leigh" is, as Mrs. Browning represents the circumstances, *physiologically impossible ?* Mrs. Browning ought to have known that a reversal of any great law of nature is beyond poetic license.

> Our Lady of the Passion, stabbed with swords
> Where the Babe sucked; or Lamia in her first
> Moonlighted pallor, ere she shrunk and blinked,
> And shuddering, wriggled down to the unclean."

What a confusion of violence is the account given of London streets and the wretched beings who dwell there :

> ". . . Faces! phew,
> We'll call them vices festering to despairs,
> Or sorrows petrifying to vices: not
> A finger-touch of God left whole in them;
> All ruined — lost — the countenance worn out
> As the garments, the will dissolute as the acts,
> The passions loose and draggling in the dirt
> To trip the foot up at the first free step!
> Those faces! 'twas as if you had stirred up hell
> To heave its lowest dreg-fiends uppermost
> In fiery swirls of slime," etc.

How much more full of meaning, to one who has seen such sights, is the simple phrase of our Laureate's, in " Maud " :

> " And I loathe the squares and streets,
> *And the faces that one meets.*"

In another passage Mrs. Browning designates the hard heart of society as —

> ". . . This social Sphinx,
> Who sits between the sepulchres and stews,
> Makes mock and mow against the crystal heavens,
> And bullies God," —

. . . Of Florence she says —

> ". . . The town, there, seems to seethe
> In this Medæan *boil-pot* of the sun,
> And all the patient hills are bubbling round
> As if a prick would leave them flat."

. . . These pieces of bad taste mainly arise from that straining after strength which mars some of the authoress's best writings ; but there are others which, in their rough treatment of themes we are accustomed to see handled with reverence, are still more repulsive. Witness the comparison of Christ to a hunter of wild beasts. In the picture of London she has so overlaid her colours, as quite to destroy the effect of what might have been a most impressive sketch. . . . Did our survey cease here, we should not be so unfair as the *Saturday Reviewer ;* but we would give the reader only some such conception of " Aurora Leigh " as he would have of the Ajax, from the bad joke on the hero's name, — of " Romeo and Juliet," from the wretched puns it contains, — of Byron's " Don Juan," from the stanzas in which he offends against delicacy, — of Wordsworth's " Idyls " from " Goody Blake and Harry Gill,"— or of Tennyson's " Maud," from the rudest of his hobbling hexameters. The worst pieces are short. The poem contains passages of concentrated beauty and sustained grandeur, enough to establish half a dozen reputations. In the presentation alike of character and scenery Mrs. Browning has proved herself in every sense a master. Those pictures of England and of Italy which so adorn the first and seventh books are already familiar to our readers ; and they will take a permanent rank among our best specimens of descriptive poetry. Some of the portraits exhibit a fund of subtle humour. Witness that oft-quoted sketch of the aunt, a lady whose temper is perhaps best represented in those three lines :

"And English women, she thanked God and sighed
(*Some people always sigh in thanking God*),
Were models to the universe."

There are many passages which we value, as much for the truth they condense as for the beauty of their language. . . . It is, however, to the general management of the poem that we must look for its main excellences, as well as for its gravest defects. . . . Romney . . . has lived near them, and seen Aurora daily, and grown to love her. She, too, loves him, unconsciously to herself, plainly enough to the reader ; but they have their own distinct views of life. He is a poet in action — she in verse. His soul is " grey with poring over the long sum of ill," — of wretchedness, and poverty, and vice, in the world around him : he has, with all the foolish enthusiasm of youth, resolved to devote his fortune and his life to lessen this ill. . . . Their interview has been compared to that famous one between Jane Eyre and St. John. There is some show of resemblance between them ; but the difference as to the essential question is infinite. St. John thought of Jane as a mere missionary ; he would as willingly have had her go with him as a sister, were it not for public opinion. Romney loves Aurora far more deeply than she deserved ; and he shows this by tone and look and gesture throughout the whole colloquy. He talks too much, perhaps, of his philanthropy, his schemes — some foolish, some as wise as any yet devised for reforming the world ; but he is diverted from superfluous display of tenderness, by the noblest thoughts of others and their welfare. . . . She, on the other hand, turns from him because she thinks too much of herself. Because he will not protest that she is born to be a poet, she distrusts and rejects his love with a most magniloquent disdain. . . . The account of her London career gives occasion for a good deal of humourous satire on

the fashionable life and talk of the metropolis. We
find nothing indeed to rival the cunning disclosures of
Thackeray; but in the fourth and fifth books there is
a large amount of vivid characterization. Some of the
minor dramatis personæ are drawn with great power;
— such as the good Lord Howe, the cautious philanthropist, never out of his depth, never honest; clever
Mister Smith, and Sir Blaise Delorme —

> " .   .   . With quiet, priest-like voice,
> Too used to syllable damnations round
> To make a natural emphasis worth while; "

and above all, Lady Waldemar — the rich, the
beautiful, the fascinating, the hateful Lady Waldemar.
. . . Stately Aurora Leigh, her theories, her speculations and her pride, — the London life, the balls,
the gossip of ladies in rustling silks, the talk of artists
and old rakes and embryo philosophers, amusing and
graphic as they are, are cast into the shade by the
apparition and the tragedy of Marian Erle. Aurora
goes to see her, and finds in the midst of one of the
wretched streets in London " an ineffable white face,"
which we get to think more beautiful than any other
in the book, —

> " .   .   . She was not white or brown,
> But could look either like a mist that changed
> According to being shone on more or less."

. . . There is nothing more exquisite in the poem
than some of the lines which refer to [the] infant. . . .
It is difficult to select; the whole . . . presents a
picture of innocence and maternal fondness such as
perhaps has never before been realized in verse, and
which reminds one more than anything else of the
masterpieces of Raphael. We confess to entertain

very different sentiments regarding the two heroines of this poem. Aurora's self-consciousness repels — her speculations do not much interest us ; her genuine human feeling is reserved for the closing scene. There is something about Marian, on the other hand, that is especially attractive. All the little incidents of her early life, the court in London, the flowers, the way she tells her tale, with the exception of one or two misplaced scientific phrases, so artless and natural, — the shrinking, clinging, half reverence, half love she feels for Romney, combine to exhibit winning beauty and grace. But nothing in the book is so grand as the revelation to Aurora of her dreadful secret — how, beguiled by the serpent kindness of the Lady Waldemar to believe herself an obstacle to Romney's happiness, committed to the charge of some female fiend, and lured into a home of horror in France, she "fell unaware, and came to butchery," doomed to live ever after subject to that law —

> "The common law by which the poor and weak
> Are trodden under foot by vicious men,
> And loathed for ever after by the good."

The tale has too deep a pathos to be expressed in any partial transcription. It is indeed a tragedy too terrible for tears. There is something almost superhuman in the awe of those concluding lines in which Marian describes her wanderings. We read them with a sort of breathless fear and wonder. . . . In an artistic point of view, this work has all the defects and all the excellences of the authoress's style. Those excellences more than counterbalance the defects. But it is a work written with an evident purpose, and it openly challenges criticism *ethically*. We cannot give a favorable verdict. . . . If, as she herself declares, "wrong thoughts make wrong poems," there is much to censure in this one. The estimate she gives of the French and the eulogy of Louis Napoleon which follows it, is a glaring evidence of a judgment easily misled by the outward shows of things, and arrested by the *semblance* of Power.

We do not intend to diverge into the field of politics to point out in what manner their "twice absolute" Emperor *represents* this "poet of the nations," or *how* "his purple is lined with the democracy." It is more within the scope of our purpose to contend with those peculiar views of reform and social philosophy which this volume has for its text. There is a widespread and growing error to which its success has given a new impulse — an error founded in a truth, perhaps, but none the less fatal. We allude to the mistake of exaggerating the effect of Art — whether as exhibited through Music, Painting, or Poetry — in ameliorating or elevating the condition of the masses of the people in any age or country. It probably results from a transference of the feelings and sympathies, which arise from or are possible only under a certain degree of culture, to spheres where that culture does not exist. But, however originating, History and our every-day experience combine to demonstrate the error. Art and the perfection of the poetic sentiments follow, or are contemporaneous with an age of prosperity. They do not constitute, nor can they supply the place of material comforts and free institutions. Artistic culture far from standing in the place of philanthropic effort, depends upon the success of that effort for its own permanence. Men must be fed, clothed, and washed, ere ever "the essential prophet's word comes in power'' to awaken, elevate, and sustain their nobler energies. . . . An attentive examination of the latter books of Mrs. Browning's poem will convince any one that we are not unjust in charging her with comparative contempt for the material agencies of civilization, and disparagement, through precept and example, of philanthropic effort. . . . It is well to know that man develops from within, that outward schemes are but imperfect methods, and that we ought not to sever poetry from the actual world. But if we doubt too much of our powers for doing good — of the possibility of lessening by enduring effort the ills around us, we fall into a profitless despair, or a false content, more truly named indifference. . . . There is . . . in the magnificent poetry at the conclusion of the book too much of the spirit of the Lotos Eaters — the most fatal, because the most fascinating form of the *laissez faire* — an acquiescence in the " Everlasting No ! '' The world would come right, we are told, if we leave it to God. *It won't.* Is it not one of the truisms of our morality, that where evil is active, good must be strenuous on all sides, or the fair fabric will go to ruin while the ministers He sent to keep it sound are singing hymns ?

Romney Leigh himself seems to be treated no less unfairly than the cause he represents. There are absurd philanthropies in abundance, pretentious schemes with no heart in them, false and idle. Had the hero of this poem advocated the most impracticable of these, his punishment had been too severe. . . . Romney Leigh for being a philanthropist, — to be rejected and lectured by his mistress — to have his intended wife stolen from him — to try everything, to succeed

in nothing — to be laughed at by everybody — to
lose his money — to have his house burned about his
ears — to get both his eyes knocked out — to beg pardon
of his old mistress at last, and confess that she was all
right and he was all wrong — to have her to take
charge of him afterwards in his mutilated state.

But Romney's schemes were not so impracticable ;
he was too good and too great a man to devote his
whole life and energy to an honest cause without some
beneficent result. He did more holy work in his
tender care and reformation of those poor girls in London than his cousin's poems could effect, were they
much better than we can imagine them to have been.
— *Westminster Review*, 1857.

Mrs. Browning takes the field like Britomart or
Joan of Arc, and declares that she will not accept
courtesy or forbearance from the critics on account of
her sex. She challenges a truthful opinion, and that
opinion she shall have. . . . The two characters, male and female, are meant to stand in strong
contrast to each other. Romney is a socialist, bent
on devoting himself to the regeneration of mankind,
and the improvement of the condition of the working
classes, by carrying into effect the schemes of Fourier
and Owen — the aim of Aurora is, through art, to
raise the aspirations of the people. The man is physical, the woman metaphysical. The one is for increas-
ing bodily comfort, the other for stimulating the mind.
Both are enthusiasts, and both are intolerably dogmatic.
. . . He has the bad taste to propose, not so
much, as he puts it, through love, but because he
wants a helpmate to assist him in the erection of
public washing-houses, soup-kitchens, and hospitals ;

whereupon our high-souled poetess flies off at a tangent. . . . The story . . . no admirer of Mrs. Browning's genius ought in prudence to defend. In our opinion it is fantastic, unnatural, exaggerated; and all the worse, because it professes to be a tale of our own times. No one who understands of how much value probability is to a tale, can read the foregoing sketch, or indeed peruse the poem, without a painful feeling that Mrs. Browning has been perpetrating, in essentials, an extravaganza or caricature, instead of giving to the public a real lifelike picture, for who can accept, as truthful representation, Romney's proposal of marriage to an ignorant uneducated girl whom he does not love; or that scene in the church, which is absolutely of Rabelaisian conception? We must not be seduced by beauty and power of execution from entering our protest against this radical error, which appears more glaring as we pass from the story to the next point, which is the delineation of character. Aurora Leigh is not an attractive character. After making the most liberal allowance for pride, and fanaticism for art, and inflexible independence, she is incongruous and contradictory both in her sentiments and in her actions. She is not a genuine woman; one-half of her heart seems bounding with the beat of humanity, while the other half is ossified. What we miss in her is instinctiveness, which is the greatest charm of women. No doubt she displays it now and then, and sometimes very conspicuously, but it is not made the general attribute of her nature; and in her dealings with Romney Leigh, instinct disappears altogether. For we hold it absolutely impossible that a woman, gifted as she is represented to be, would have countenanced a kinsman, whom she respected only, in the desperate folly of wedding an uneducated girl from the lowest grade of society, whom he did not love, simply for the sake of a theory ; thereby making himself a public laughing-stock, without the least chance of advancing the progress of his own preposterous opinions. There is nothing heroic in this ; there is nothing reconcilable with duty. The part which Aurora takes in the transaction, degrades rather than raises her in our eyes ; nor is she otherwise thoroughly amiable ; for, with all deference to Mrs. Browning, and with ideas of our own perhaps more chivalric than are commonly promulgated, we must maintain that woman was created to be dependent on the man, and not in the primary sense his lady and his mistress. The extreme independence of Aurora detracts from the feminine charm, and mars the interest which we otherwise might have felt in so intellectual a heroine. In fact, she is made to resemble too closely some of the female portraits of George Sand, which never were to our liking. In Romney we fail to take any kind of interest. Though honorable and generous, he is such a very decided noodle that we grudge him his prominence in the poem, do not feel much sympathy for his misfortunes, and cannot help wondering that Aurora should have entertained one spark of affection for so deplorable a milksop. Excess of enthusiasm we can allow ; and folly, affecting to talk the words of wisdom, meets us at every turning ; but Romney is a walking hyperbole. The character of Marian is very beautifully drawn and well-sustained, but her thoughts and language are not those of a girl reared in the midst of sordid poverty, vice, and ignorance. This is an error in art which we are sure Mrs. Browning, upon mature consideration, will acknowledge ; and it might

easily have been avoided by the simple expedient
of making Marian's origin and antecedents a few shades
more respectable, which still would have left enough
disparity between her and Romney to produce the
effect which Mrs. Browning desires. Lady Waldemar is a disgusting character. Mrs. Browning intended her to appear as despicable ; but it was not,
therefore, necessary to make her talk coarse and revolting. . . . Anything very hideous or revolting
taints the air around it, and produces a sensation of
loathing, from which we do not immediately recover.
Hence poets, even when their situations are of the
most tragic nature — even when they are dealing
with subjects questionable in morality — do, for the
most part, sedulously avoid anything like coarseness of
expression, and frame their language so as to convey
the general idea without presenting special images
which are calculated to disgust. Indeed, whilst
reading this poem, which abounds in references to art,
we have been impressed with a doubt whether, with
all her genius, accomplishment, and experience, Mrs.
Browning has ever thought seriously of the principles
upon which art is founded. For genius, as we all
know, or ought to know, is not of itself sufficient for
the construction of a great poem. Artists, like archi-
tects, must work by rule — not slavishly indeed, but
ever keeping in mind that there are certain principles
which experience has tested and approved, and that
to deviate from these is literally to court defeat. . . .
In the fifth book of this poem there is a dissertation
upon poetry, in which Mrs. Browning very plainly
indicates her opinion that the chief aim of a poet
should be to illustrate the age in which he lives. . . .
This, in our apprehension, would lead to a total sacri-

fice of the ideal. It is not the province of the poet to depict things as they are, but so to refine and purify as to purge out the grosser matter ; and this he cannot do if he attempts to give a faithful picture of his own times. For, in order to be faithful, he must necessarily include much which is abhorrent to art and revolting to the taste, for which no exactness of delineation will be accepted as a proper excuse. All poetical characters, all poetical situations, must be idealized. . . . In this poem she has wilfully alternated passages of sorry prose with bursts of splendid poetry. . . . We have already said that the character of Marian Erle is beautifully drawn and well sustained, and yet it is the humblest of them all. But in depicting her, Mrs. Browning has abstained from all meanness. If she errs at all, it is by making the girl appear more refined in thought and expression than is justified by her previous history, but that is an error on the safe side, and one which may be readily excused. Marian, little better than a pariah-girl, does undoubtedly attract our sympathies more than the polished and high-minded Aurora, the daughter of a noble race — not certainly as the bride of Romney, but as the mother of a hapless child. There, indeed, Mrs. Browning has achieved a triumph ; for never yet — no, not in her " Cry of the Children," one of the most pathetic and tear-stirring poems in the English language — has she written anything comparable to the passages which refer to Marian and her babe. . . . If we have not been able conscientiously to praise the story, either as regards conception or execution, no such restriction is laid upon us while dealing with isolated passages. Mrs. Browning possesses in a very high degree the faculty of description, presenting us often with the most brilliantly coloured pictures. In this respect, if we may be allowed to institute such a comparison, she resembles Turner, being sometimes even extravagant in the vividness of her tints. . . . Nor is the great genius of Mrs. Browning less conspicuous in other portions of the poem which relate to the natural affections. Once and again, whilst perusing this volume, have we experienced a sensation of regret that one so admirably gifted should have wasted much of her power upon what are, after all, mere artistic experiments. . . . We could wish — though wishes avail not for the past — that Mrs. Browning had selected a more natural and intelligible theme, which would have given full scope for the display of her extraordinary powers ; and we trust that she will yet reconsider her opinion as to the abstract fitness for poetical use of a subject illustrative of the times in which we live. It may be that there is no difficulty which genius cannot conquer ; at the same time we cannot commend the wisdom of those who go out of their way on purpose to search for difficulties. . . . We cannot allow fancy to be trammelled in its work by perpetual reference to realities. Still, with all its faults, this is a remarkable poem, strong in energy, rich in thought, abundant in beauty.— *Blackwood's Magazine,* 1857.

THE main object of this work . . . is, we take it, to deal with some of the great social questions of our own day through the powerful vehicle of poetry, as Kingsley and others have done in prose. The lesson that is most prominently taught we conceive to be this, that no social reform can be successful which seeks to obliterate class distinctions by fusing them one into the other — a truth which we should think sufficiently obvious to every reflecting mind. Concurrent with this runs the illustration of woman's life, in its social suffering and in its highest intellectual development ; and beneath both, in the failure both of Romney and Aurora to work out to a prosperous issue their own theories, is finally exhibited, to an extent, perhaps, beyond what the author intended, the utter dependence of each sex upon the other, the truth that if a primæval decree gave man the dominion, it was as much for woman's happiness as his own — a dominion which the holy principle of love turns into a blessing to both, by making obedience an anticipating assent. "Bowing beneath that law which sounded through the darkening paradise, she wins for her dower the only freedom that is worthy of woman — the moral liberty which God bestows upon the faithful and obedient spirit." . . . We look upon such a moral portraiture as that of Marian Erle almost monstrous in its faultlessness, and cannot pronounce it true to nature ; and yet the power and beauty with which Mrs. Browning has wrought out the picture fascinates one's gaze, and makes us forget all that is unreal in our admiration of all that is rich in the colouring and forcible in the expression. The story of Marian Erle is plainly designed by the authoress as an illustration of the results of class oppression, and class suffering. . . . The throng of the people in their deepest degradation and wretchedness, the outpourings of lanes and alleys, these are pourtrayed with a masculine vigour, and somewhat of a masculine coarseness of touch, . . . extravagant indeed beyond the very limits of probability, but powerful and stirring, notwithstanding the sense of the unreal that

accompanies the reader throughout.   Aurora pursues
her poetic course and delivers herself entirely to its
study.   The fifth book may be said to consist of the
views of a poet upon the subject of art in general,
especially in connection with poetry.   Here Mrs.
Browning rises to the highest elevation.   Profound
thoughts, fine criticism, a noble, just, passionate appreciation of poetry, all poured out in a flood of rich,
felicitous language, sparkling with illustrations, and
glowing as if blood-hot from the heart, tell at once
that we have the writer revealed to us here in her
own nature. . . .   In the midst of all this high thinking, we have interposed a scene in a fashionable London ball-room as prosaic and inane as can well be
imagined.   With this we are not disposed to quarrel ;
on the contrary, we think it has been introduced with
an artistic purpose and design to produce high effect
by strong contrast.   We find the same thing, again
and again, done by Shakespeare, in " Hamlet," in the
"Tempest," in " Lear," and elsewhere.   The coarse
or foolish, or the low in thought and expression, following quickly upon the elevated and poetic.   We see it
in great paintings, as in the Marriage at Cana, where,
amidst the magnificence of regal splendour, the dog
laps up viands from a golden dish.   We see it, in fine,
in real life,— the commonplace and prosaic ever touching upon but not blending with the sublime and poetic,
like colours which set off each other when in juxtaposi-
tion, but do not lose their distinctive characters by
fusion.   Such a fusion the author might easily have
effected by clothing the sentiments of the ball-room
men and women in poetic language ; but she would
then have been neither true to their nature nor to her
own art, and we hold very cheaply the superficial

criticism that condemns this episode in "Aurora Leigh." . . . Let us now look at the work as a whole, unaffected if possible by the affluence and splendour of diction and imagery and thought which may be found throughout it. From what point of view are we to regard this singular production? In what category of writings are we to class it? Is it a poetic novel of real life, or a poetic romance — fiction embodying and exhibiting mere theories of life and speculations upon art, in unreal actors? If we take the latter to be the true statement, we can bear with complacency what is exaggerated, unreal, and extravagant, as we endure without complaint the supernatural heroes and the mist-inflated, giant warriors of Homer and Ossian. But on the other hand, if we are to apply to it the test of real life we are met at every step by incongruities. The character of Romney Leigh is exaggerated and unnatural; weak and almost silly at times; impractical in his schemes of social regeneration, and absurd in his theories; a modern Quixote, more mad than the errant knight who assailed windmills and slaughtered sheep; and with all this is mixed a nobility of nature and a grandeur of sentiment that make him, as a whole, a moral monster. Marian Erle presents, we believe, no true type of a class, either in the high moral or intellectual attributes with which she is invested, or in the sufferings which she endures. Undoubtedly the character of Aurora Leigh is developed with more truth to nature than any other in the book. Here we have indeed the woman in the attainment of her full stature of mind; but throughout the thoughts and feelings to which she gives expression, there runs a jealous and morbid sense of the misappreciation of woman by man, a "struggling for woman's empery," and even for something beyond it. . . . Indeed, in the effort to stand, not on a pedestal beside man, but actually to occupy his place, we see Mrs. Browning commit grave errors. She assumes, as it were, the gait and the garb of man, but the stride and the strut betray her. She is occasionally coarse in expression and unfeminine in thought ; and utters what, if they be even truths, are so conveyed that we would hesitate to present them to the eye of the readers of her own sex. There is nothing that detracts so much from the pleasure which the perusal of this poem has given us, as this conviction, that the authoress has written a book which is almost a closed volume for her own sex. . . . Thoughtful, philosophic, vigourous and tender, with a passion and an earnestness that carry her right on to her object and sustain her throughout, her criticism as an artist and a poet is rarely at fault. Her appreciation of natural beauties is intense, and her power of describing them as great, we believe, as that of any living poet. The scenes glow beneath her pencil. Nor is her power of tracing and exhibiting the intellectual processes inferior ; and one feels that the mysteries of the mind are as thoughtfully expatiated upon by her quick and sagacious spirit as are all the poetries which abound in the material world. Be the faults what they may in conception or in execution, we almost forget them in the charm of the language, and the thoughts which surprise and delight us everywhere. — *Dublin University Magazine*, 1857.

THERE was always something of the Titaness about Mrs. Browning : her instincts were towards the vague, the vast, the indefinite, the unutterable ; and the ideal world in which her imagination lived was a world of formless grandeur, of radiant mist, in which shapes of superhuman majesty moved and loomed dimly glorious. In her art she was a Pythoness struggling for utterance, too full of the god to do more than writhe her lips in convulsed agony ; her speech was inarticulate, often because she meant so much ; the note she sounded became a hollow noise, because it was so deep. In this state of mind she wrote lyrical dramas on the Fall of Man and the Crucifixion of Christ, which were little more than hysterical spasms ; poured herself forth in improvisations which in one stanza stirred every heart and thrilled every soul, and in the next moved inextinguishable laughter, so strangely were strength and weakness mingled, grand thought and deep feeling with nonsense, affectation, and wilful puerility. "Casa Guidi Windows" was a great advance, though still there was much to do before she became mistress of her own powers — before she could guide the mental coursers of her chariot with a light finger on the silken reins of art. "Aurora Leigh" is in point of execution another step forward ; if the steeds still toss their heads somewhat wildly for well-bred carriage-horses, still snuff the air as if the trackless desert were their native home, it is that their mistress prefers to drive with a loose rein, and would rather ride with Mazeppa than take a ticket by the Great Western or a canter round Rotten Row.

But the old anarchic nature of the Titaness is still discernible ; still there is something of the old contempt for limitation and the littleness of completeness ; still the conception vast and vague and only half realized ; rich elements of force and beauty in chaos and confusion, the waters heaving and boiling with life ere yet the demiurgic spirit has brooded over them, and given to each thing its definite form and its separate place. The poem professes to be the autobiography of a woman of genius, who early in life refuses to marry a man she likes, because he, being a philanthropist, seems to her to seek her for his wife not so much as a woman whom he loves, and whose love he wants, as to be his helper in his social work. She is further offended by his slight estimate of art and literature, and by his disbelief in a woman's ability to attain high excellence in either. So far as concerns herself, the record is one more of feelings than of facts, a history of mental growth and the development of character rather than of fortune and outward incidents. But there is no lack of incidents, and those of so startling a character that they might serve for the plot of a Victoria melodrama. Indeed, nothing can be more evident than that Mrs. Browning has not cared to throw an air of every-day probability over her story, or to propitiate in the least that sort of refinement which avoids almost with equal horror violent emotions and eccentric actions. The two principal characters in the book, besides the autobiographer, Aurora Leigh, are her cousin, Romney Leigh, whom she refuses to marry for the motives before assigned, and a girl of the lowest station, named Marian Erle, who is pure and good, though abjectly poor and the child of brutal tramps. There are other characters incidentally introduced, one of whom, a fashionable young widow, Lady Waldemar, plays a leading part in the development of the story ; but the three we have mentioned are the dramatis personæ, and it is in their mutual relations that the interest of the poem consists. Thus we have already two very distinct elements of poetic excitement in the growth of Aurora's character, in her experience as woman and artist, and in the strange fortunes of Romney Leigh and Marian Erle. But along with these, we have on the one hand, as appropriate enough to Aurora's autobiography, frequent discursive reflections on art and life in general, sketches of people in society, the brilliant talk of London evening-parties, and all that might naturally enter into the journalizing of a literary woman mixing the literary and fashionable society of London ; and on the other, as Romney Leigh is a philanthropist to begin with, and loses his wife through an overstraining on the practical side of life and marriage, he too passes through the various phases of socialistic opinion ; and the book not only abounds in discussion and allusions to the various and conflicting theories and schemes for the regeneration of society, but its deepest object consists, we should say, in the contrast and final reconcilement of Aurora's artistic cultivation of the individual, with Romney's mechanical and materialistic plans for the improvement of the masses. It would require not perhaps more genius and intellect than Mrs. Browning has shown to organize all this material, all these elements, into a poem of which each part should grow from the expanding life of the central idea, and be necessary to the completeness of the whole ; but it would require a more patient endurance of intellectual toil, a more resolute hand upon the reins, more thought, more pains, less self-indulgences in composition, less wilfulness. She has succeeded in writing brilliantly and powerfully almost throughout this long poem of more than ten thousand lines of blank verse ; she has touched social problems with the light of her penetrating intellect and the warmth of her

passionate heart ; has painted scenery with a free outline and a glowing colour ; has sketched characters as
a sensitive and observant woman can sketch them ;
above all, she has dramatized passion with a force and
energy that recall the greatest masters of tragedy :
but these various excellences, though they make a
book interesting and prove genius of a high order, do
not make a great poem, and will never be held to do
so by any persons who know and feel that a work of
art is something different in kind from the finest discursive talk, or even from a collection of studies however masterly, and though they may be ingeniously
patchworked into a cleverly-devised frame.

It may be that Mrs. Browning cares little for this
distinction ; and that she would tell us that, provided
the wine be good, the shape of the glass matters not —
that she never aimed at writing a great poem in our
sense of the word, but only at writing fine sense and
deep feeling. Be it so, if she really is satisfied with
that explanation. We do not understand an artist
who ignores art, especially when the consciousness of
high moral and artistic aims is evidently present, and
only the patient effort, the resolute will to conquer
difficulties, is wanting. For the rest, she has succeeded
in saying a number of beautiful things in a free and
natural manner, that loses little of its ease and lightness
in the more prosaic parts of the poem, and gains in
much larger proportion in the impassioned parts by
being in verse. . . . The essential fault of this book
is that the plan is too large and complex for the mental
power brought to bear upon it ; that the characters do
not sufficiently act upon each other, and are too sta-
tionary in their own development. They neither
grow from mutual influence nor from the expansion of

their own individuality. Aurora is much the same person at thirty as at twenty; the accident which finally brings about the dénouement would have brought it at any period in her mental growth. Marian Erle is a statue of heroic goodness, out of whom circumstances bring the varying expressions of that goodness, but who can scarcely be said to change, to learn anything, to develop powers or virtues though she manifests them. And Romney Leigh is a somewhat vaguely-conceived type of a particular kind of self-sacrifice and intellectual narrowness, invested with the outward form and circumstances of an English gentleman. . . . We do not know whether Mrs. Browning has ever read "Clarissa Harlowe," Mrs. Gaskell's "Ruth," and Miss Brontë's "Jane Eyre;" but in the story of Marian Erle she has joined together the central incident of "Clarissa Harlowe" with the leading sentiment of "Ruth"— that healing and reconciling influence of the maternal passion for a child whose birth is, according to common worldly feeling, the mother's disgrace. The combination is striking and original, not to say courageous in a lady. We mention it to disavow any feeling of repugnance to the moral, though we certainly do question the propriety and good taste of introducing the "Clarissa Harlowe" calamity under any amount of reserve, or for any emotional effect, in poem or novel. The bar of the Old Bailey is the only place where we wish to hear of such things. The same objection does not of course apply to the incident borrowed from "Jane Eyre." But it is disagreeable to be so forcibly reminded of a recent and popular work, when a small expenditure of ingenuity would have avoided the resemblance; which is enhanced by the fact that the incident proves in each case the solution of the story's knot.— *The Spectator*, 1857.

Mrs. Browning . . . was unquestionably a woman of rare genius, if that term can with propriety be applied to an excess of ardent irregular power.   She had also learning and power of thought ; but she was entirely deficient in the highest gifts of her own art.   She had neither simplicity, taste, or good sense.   Her style was always inflated ; and her fame would be ten times as great and as deserved as it is, if she had left us a single lucid and finished performance, instead of a crowd of incoherent thoughts and extravagant images. . . .   She appears to have written to please herself, with little care of the unpleasant feelings which are excited in the minds of others by distorted conceits and mean and often ridiculous versification.   She is often more quaint than Quarles in her imagery, more grotesque than Cowley or Donne in her ideas, more eccentric in her rhymes than the author of " Hudibras," and often more coarsely masculine than any known female writer.   She invests inanimate objects and abstractions with human features which make pure nonsense.   " The rose lifts up her white hand."   Eternity smiles with dim grand lips ! A mystery has a knee !   The dark has a lap.   Wonders breathe.   The earth wields a sceptre, and the " Universe shakes dew-drops from its mane like a roused lion."   " Aurora Leigh " is a rank unweeded garden of the most intolerable conceits. . . .   Due allowance, therefore, being made for these strange defects, it stands beyond doubt that much as Mrs. Browning sank at times below the commonest demands of harmony and expression, yet that no woman has ever handled the English tongue with greater force and spirit when she is at her best. . . . Upon the first appearance of "Aurora Leigh," the daring novelty and vehemence of particular passages veiled its many deformities and faults of construction, the prosaic baldness of much of the narrative, its distorted ingenuity, the harsh discordances, the transitions, elaborate conceits and grotesqueness of much of the dialogue, the utter impossibility of the story, and the unreality of all its actors. But a return to its pages dispels the reader's illusions, and he is compelled to regard it as a splendid failure in an impossible attempt. The whole of the interest of the story consists in the intellectual and moral development of two personages, both of whom are projections of Mrs. Browning's own nature; and their views about art and about life are such as Mrs. Browning herself may be supposed to have held at different points of her career. The history of these two chief persons is embarrassed with many indelicate and inconceivable incidents, and interwoven with the actions of other men and women of less interest and less truth of character than those for whose sake they are introduced. The romance, so far as it is a novel, is utterly bad, and only redeemed from ridicule by the occasional bursts of impassioned diction which it contains. We do not dispute that "Aurora Leigh" contains evidence of originality and power, but even those gifts do not produce a poem in the absence of that judgment and taste which Mrs. Browning certainly did not acquire from her classical studies. It is remarkable that a mind trained, as hers had been, in the love of Greek literature, should have been utterly devoid of the chaste, correct, and finished beauty of Greek art. . . . Considering the great capabilities she possessed, her career may be accepted as some proof of the impossibility that women can ever attain to the first rank in imaginative composition. Such a combination of the finest genius and the choicest results of cultivation and wide-ranging studies has never been seen before in any woman, nor is the world likely soon to see the same again. — *Edinburgh Review*, October, 1861.

WE have read no modern poem more full of thought, that stirs the blood, quickens the pulse and makes it leap. At times we pause and listen, for the notes of Aurora are not always clear. Why should they be ? — this mild Florentine, with the smell of oleanders on her wings, and her heart all full of snatches from the Tuscan groves ; full-throated, she can scarcely pant them out without, at times, tripping each other's heels. We sometimes say either the poet must be dazzled or we are. Well, we read her again and it is all clear. The fault is in us, not in her. Often have we known that the reader must be *en rapport* with such poets, or they can not be understood. Never read " Aurora Leigh " when your head is weak from too full a stomach, or dyspeptic, — better read Japanese. Whether it is that we cannot see the pebbles shining at the bottom of this tarn, or so shallow that the pebbles have no shining, we cannot, at times, say ; but it is certain that, like the great cosmos, it has its riddles, mysteries, morasses, deserts, fogs, and fens ; but for all these it is God's cosmos.

This " Aurora Leigh " is a great poem. It is a wonder of art. It will live. No large audience will it have, but it will have audience ; and that is more than most poems have. To those who know what poetry is and in what struggles it is born — how the great thoughts justify themselves — this work will be looked upon as one of the wonders of the age.

We say "Aurora Leigh" will live, not by special grant of the great public, for this will not know that such a thing has dawned upon it. The day dawns upon us, not because we will, but because the sun wills. It will not be by grant of the king or the senate, or because of tinted paper and gold, but because "it is a thing of beauty and a joy forever!" It is one withal that has in it life and cannot perish. It is sometimes quaint, as the oaks of Wordsworth's:

> "... Those fraternal four of Bowerdale
> Joined in one solemn and capacious grove
> Of intertwisted fibres, serpentine,
> Up-coiling, and inveterately convolved —
> Nor uninformed of phantasy and looks
> That threaten the profane!"

This book could not have been written when "Prometheus Bound" and her earlier works were wrought. These, like all works from the great masters, were but the froth and bubbles tossing on that sea which alone could have produced them, but which, at best, were froth and bubbles, not the sea. She did not know until Aurora arose what daylight was, what the sun could do, what glory it casts upon the breezy trees and the slumberous earth, the sea and its multitudinous waves. . . . In all her previous contributions, the same original, self-poised mind appears at times, but in none of them does it stand out so fully and so clearly as in "Aurora Leigh;" and hence its superiority to anything written by her pen. She lost sight of old dead forms. No longer the mocking bird, — if indeed she ever was — but now the lark, upspringing from the dewy grass, she flings her arrows, clear and keen. . . . Just two lines we quote, for their singular strength and sublimity, with reference to death — the death of her father :

> " . . . Life, struck sharp on death,
> Makes awful lightning." . . .

Many such short, Shakespearian sentences may be found in this work, which will pass into the common speech, as they can never be forgotten. We deem this to be one of the triumphs of poetry. It fulfils its office in those words which linger in the memory, and enter into the life of all this busy, bustling world. . . . The uncommon force and felicity with which Mrs. Browning expresses her thoughts are not the least of her excellencies. She has a rich vocabulary — a large utterance, never at a loss for the right word in the right place. This strikes the reader throughout the entire work. She is not always smooth or even in the flow of her language, as Wordsworth, nor is she tame, as he sometimes is, in the medium through which she chooses to give expression to her conceptions of truth. Never cramped by system, as though poetry had a language solely its own, but in the largeness of her ideal she deals with the world of art as God does in nature. Sometimes rugged, disjointed, abrupt, throwing up her mountain masses as fiery sparks, letting down the awful avalanche, with the thunder which follows it ; and then, as the river flowing "at its own sweet will" through open glades and towering trees, castles and broken towers, now spreading out over the marsh-moor, then compressed between the jaws of mountains, ready to devour it. In any phase of thought, finding, without effort, apparently, words which convey their own music, independent of the thoughts which they utter. . . . We have said "Aurora Leigh" should not be read, but studied deeply, meditatively. We know of no better work for the youthful mind, filled with lofty aspirations, to pore over, than this. If one wishes to know the stuff that poets are made of, the things that they endure, the struggles to reach a purer life, the patience and the toil to attain it, the self-abnegation needful, the world of thought and feeling to which they are admitted, ere they see in the desert the sphinx with sober face, — the sounding of that desert ere they catch a full sight of the presiding spirit which dwells there, the failures, the praise which means scorn, the blame which is often the highest praise, the self-reliance in a world where none can stand alone, let them read "Aurora Leigh"! — *J. Challen in National Quarterly Review, 1862.*